For Every Season

For Every Season

Reflective Liturgies for Worship

Anastasia Somerville-Wong

THE
PILGRIM
PRESS
Cleveland

I am grateful to my husband,
Gerald Wong,
to whom I dedicate this book,
for his constant friendship, support, and love

The Pilgrim Press
700 Prospect Avenue
Cleveland, Ohio 44115
thepilgrimpress.com

Library of Congress Cataloging-in-Publication Data
Somerville-Wong, Anastasia, 1982-
    For every season : reflective liturgies for worship /
Anastasia Somerville-Wong.
        pages   cm
    Includes bibliographical references.
    ISBN 978-0-8298-1936-6 (alk. paper)
    1. Worship programs. I. Title.
BV198.S55 2013
264–dc23   2013004037

Contents

v

Acknowledgments

I would like to thank The Pilgrim Press acquisitions committee and Kim Sadler for seeing the potential in these liturgies, Darlene Grant and the rest of the marketing team, and John Eagleson for typesetting the manuscript, and converting my work to an American style in punctuation, spelling, and grammar.

I am grateful to those who have written endorsements for my book, and also to the Reverend Brian Hilsley, minister of Wardie Parish Church, Edinburgh, and Reverend Dr. Anne Logan, minister of Stockbridge Parish Church, Edinburgh, for their willingness to host services in which these liturgies could begin to be used.

Introduction

Christians make up more of the world's population than any other religious or secular group. Moreover, the faith is experiencing growth in numbers unparalleled by any other religion, except perhaps for Islam, though the difficulties in obtaining accurate statistics for conversions make it impossible to be exact. With over 2.1 billion followers worldwide (about one-third of the world's total human population), compared to Islam's 1.5 billion and the 1.1 billion who have an entirely secular worldview, Jesus is the world's favorite religious figure, sought after for spiritual and moral direction.

The future of theology, our conceptions of God, and the life and teachings of the church should therefore matter to all of us, whether we are religious or atheistic in our worldview, since it will not only help shape private lives or even the collective future of the largest portion of humanity but will have an increasingly global impact on public life, including the social, economic, and political. In the light of the rapid growth and new expressions within Christian faith communities across the world, it is an exciting time to be a Christian and an important time to make one's contribution to what we hope will be a brighter and better future.

We are living through a period of change as revolutionary as our predecessors experienced during what became known as the Reformation. It was the scent of these changes, especially the flowering of modern progressive-minded expressions of the faith, that inspired me to write this book, with the desire to play my part in helping present and future generations to continue to live out their faith in worship and community, without compromising their intellects or their moral integrity.

This book is a complete collection of progressive liturgies and meditations for churches, small groups, family worship, and personal devotion. As a collection it provides answers to two important questions: Why do we need religion, and how should we practice it? Although I address these within the context of Christianity, many of the points made are equally applicable to other religions. It is by observing and comparing the practices and theologies of different religions that some general conclusions can be reached in answer to the these questions. Thus, comparative religion is one of the most important scholarly endeavors of our time.

The book draws on my own observations and experience of many different religious expressions, in order to outline what religion is or should be about. It considers the potential of religion to enrich and strengthen our understanding of morality and justice, to help us to find healing and peace, to build community around a shared identity, history, mission, stories, and rituals. It explores the power of religion to raise aspirations and to transform lives through aspects of salvation such as healing, liberation, enlightenment, and epiphany.

It reveals how religion can be an exhilarating lifelong quest for meaning and purpose, truth and learning, as we dwell on the complexities and conundrums of life, just as the Hebrew scribes did in the writing of Job and Ecclesiastes. It also considers the necessity for religion to deal with our psychological needs at different stages of life, especially at pivotal moments such as birth, coming of age, marriage, death, and bereavement.

Our changing psychological states have an enormous influence on what kind of religion (or secular philosophy) we choose to follow or what kind of church we choose to attend at a particular time. Their impact is often greatly underestimated and people's resulting religious commitments mistaken, by themselves or others, for reasoned belief or unreasonable folly. It was therefore of the utmost importance that these liturgies would address our emotional and psychological needs as broadly as possible, without compromising an overarching rational integrity, since a relevant faith is a faith that is sympathetic to the hopes and fears of ordinary people.

Why Liturgy?

There has always been something irresistible about the capturing of faith in poetry and in words spoken in unison. It was, after all, the regular reciting of liturgies which for many centuries passed on the foundations and framework of Christian faith and worship from one generation to the next, not only before the invention of the printing press but even after Bibles, tracts and pamphlets became widely available and great advances in literacy were made.

Liturgies help to preserve the key insights of a religious tradition through the ages. As a congregation grows familiar with the words through repetition, they become the owners of those words, individually and then collectively as a church. The liturgy reinforces a sense of common ownership and responsibility for the whole church—its building, its message, and its direction. Once liturgies are widespread, they give travelers and migrants the sense that they belong to a global community as they find those familiar words and the sentiments they convey wherever they are in the world.

Liturgies, alongside Christian songs, hymns, and sermons, are vital in shaping the faith, vision, and religious life of a Christian community or congregation both corporately and on an individual basis. They bring Christian education out of the schoolroom and hall theater and into the local churches and family homes, making the journey of faith once more a truly communal experience.

Writing a book of liturgies which can develop and nurture a modern theology that is both credible and life transformative in terms of spiritual and moral character seemed more worthwhile than adding to the already sufficient numbers of theological and philosophical tomes that will be read only by the scholarly few.

What are really needed are creative and inspirational materials that facilitate the living and practice of a progressive and unapologetically radical understanding of the Christian way that is appropriate for the twenty-first century. The liturgies in this book are intended to demonstrate that such resources do not need to sacrifice any beauty of expression or subtlety in meaning to accomplish this task.

One of the criticisms levied at the use of liturgies is that because of their set words and patterns of worship they serve only to entrench theology and dogma and limit the variety of expressions open to worshipers rather than encouraging freedom of thought and practice. It is indeed possible for liturgies to have this effect, as they have helped to inhibit both diversity and progress in the past. However, as I hope this book will demonstrate, they also have the power to establish and safeguard a more flexible and open-minded theology, while maintaining a humility that allows for change, without losing the power of the Christian message and its original insights. These liturgies are also for use, not in place of, but in conjunction with other forms of worship and practice; indeed, they encourage such complementary activities.

The Theology

The collection of liturgies in this book provides a broader, more inclusive theological content and structure for corporate worship than is generally available. The liturgies are informed and inspired by modern biblical interpretation but also by the much greater understanding of reality which we have gained through the sciences and wider literature and from our knowledge of the long history of Christianity with its myriad expressions throughout the world. They therefore take a serious but not necessarily literal approach to the Bible and embrace a more interpretive, metaphorical, and nuanced understanding of the diverse legend, ballad, history, story, and law book biblical texts, with consideration for their context and collation.

They reveal a fresh view of the place and authority of the Bible in our religion. There is respect for reason as well as paradox and mystery, rather than a blind allegiance to right doctrines or dogmas, and throughout they show a willingness to question tradition and to seek to maintain intellectual integrity. Furthermore, the liturgies encourage a proactive search to discover and uncover the truth, even when it may be uncomfortable or inconvenient. The liturgies seek to find God in a broader revelation that can be found in secular literature, art, poetry, dance, music, crafts, and the teachings and artistic achievements of other religious traditions so that these become a source of wisdom and inspiration in addition to Christian scriptures. To deny the presence of God in the wider world is to deny the work of the Holy Spirit of God through human history and creativity and in the natural world, and to confine the divine presence to our own limited sphere.

The liturgies place their emphasis on salvation here and now, in the form of both physical liberation from oppression and spiritual transformation (either incremental or epiphanous) instead of the more traditional focus on collecting brownie points in either religious or moral actions or statements of belief in the hope that, when we die, they will allow us safe passage through the gates of heaven and an escape from frightening visions of hell and eternal punishment. There is also a stress on the social and corporate aspects of sin and salvation, as well as the personal, and consequently the importance of upholding social justice as integral to Christian discipleship. The liturgies also demonstrate strong ecological concerns and commitments, emphasizing the environmental stewardship of the earth as integral to Christian discipleship.

Throughout the liturgies is an emphasis on orthopraxy over orthodoxy, right actions over right belief. Divine immanence too is reflected in the words as much as if not more than divine transcendence, affirming the presence of God in the natural world and in humanity, with a leaning toward panentheism rather than supernatural theism. However, there is frequent acknowledgment that God is both within and beyond creation; that God remains more than and better than the measurable reality our finite minds can grasp and that there are grave dangers in identifying the divine with humanity too closely.

There is a deliberate absence in the liturgies of the claim that Christianity is the only valid way to connect with God. Strongly present, on the other hand, is the affirmation of the Christian faith as saving and enlightening, while a sincere respect for other faiths is maintained. There is evident throughout a celebration of human diversity, which avoids the stereotyping of groups according to gender, sexual orientation, ethnicity, education, and economic background. Discipleship rather than membership is encouraged to avoid rigid categories of insiders and outsiders, and to create the mental space and social environment for the flourishing of less conditional affections.

Most importantly, the liturgies emphasize the power and centrality of love, compassion, and moral and spiritual transformation in the Christian faith. They encourage vitality, movement, and the expression of diverse personalities, inviting participation in arts-infused and poetic worship. They embrace the use of spiritual rituals, emphasizing the importance of sacrament (physical events as vehicles for spiritual events) and contemplative practices such as meditation.

They use drama and ritual to harness sacramental truths and contemporary practices such as meditation to focus and sharpen the mind. The liturgies incorporate many suggestions for physical acts of worship which members of the congregation can choose either to participate in or to observe and reflect upon. Sometimes these are innovative, encouraging that unending creativity necessary for conveying the Christian message both relevantly and evocatively.

Others I hope breathe new life into older practices which have become tired rituals and appear to be irrelevant because their meaning has been obscured or forgotten.

The liturgies are designed to reflect a kind of Christianity that eagerly involves itself in the messy and uncertain reality of life, willing to make the difficult choices, unafraid to risk failure, unperturbed by a few mistakes or disappointments, one which puts aside its pride and false piety and risks getting its hands dirty in politics and confrontations in the interests of justice and peace. It is the kind of Christianity which is willing, like the scientist, to make the experiment and learn from the results as they come in, a kind of Christianity that evolves by adapting to its changing environment with cheerfulness and an enduring trust in the overarching purposes of God.

Through these liturgies, I endeavor to outline a vision for church as an inspiring meeting space, a community of friendship, and a center of learning and creativity, in which personal and social development, and all the ingredients for a good life, may reach their fullest potential. It reflects my own renewed hope for a Christian future, stemming from a deep conviction that many of the teachings and practices of more than two thousand years of Christian history, even when looked at through the lens of our contemporary knowledge of science and psychology, contain truths, insights, and lessons to be learned that are still relevant and have the potential to profoundly enrich our lives in the present and future.

At the center of this abundance of inherited theology, history, and tradition, of course, is the wisdom and example of the Jewish carpenter named Jesus. The liturgies in this book, though intentionally innovative in their theological profile and pioneering in their application to worship, draw together the strands of our Christian inheritance of which we can rightfully be proud, and maintain a strong connection with our Christian past.

All human beings have attributes and talents that God calls for them to express with their best efforts as far as their circumstances allow. For many, it is religion: the stories passed from one generation to another by word of mouth, or written down in manuscripts that become scripture, which motivate and compel them to apply their personal and material resources to transform the world around them for better or worse.

Christians are distinct in that their greatest spiritual resource is not only a book of scriptures, disciplines such as fasting, praying, or obeying religious law, a spiritual gift such as the ability to preach or prophesy, or even an oral tradition of storytelling or liturgy. Uniquely, it is something less prescribed or predictable: a person, Jesus, who is seen to be the supreme revelation of God among humankind. Christianity is at root a personality cult. For a small number of first-century Jews, Jesus became the fullest personal manifestation of the impersonal, unnamable God, the God who said to Moses, "I am who I am" (Exod. 3:14), that they had ever known.

The Bible reveals a constant struggle to describe the indescribable God. It does not pretend to have all the answers; indeed, its prophets repeatedly rise up against the clerics and traditionalists of their day, and the Bible tells stories like those of Job and Jonah which are unashamedly fictional accounts exploring open-endedly the theological mysteries and conundrums they were wrestling with. A great and enduring paradox was created between the conception of God in the dominant Greek elite culture, the perfect and unchanging God of Plato, and Jesus, the apex of Judaism's passionate conception of a constantly intervening deity who demanded obedience and punished disloyalty, giving meaning and explanation for the recurrent misfortunes of their people.

These internal conflicts sparked nearly two centuries of debate over which books should be included in the Bible and five centuries of debate surrounding the nature of such central things as the Incarnation and the Trinity. This early variety is no doubt the reason for Christianity's remarkable and continuing ability to reinvent itself through the ages and in so many different contexts around the globe. It was political circumstances and privileged elites which gradually decided upon these issues for the majority of Christians at councils such as Chalcedon in 451, but there were always significant dissenting minorities.

The Bible is important primarily because it is the major source-book for our knowledge of Jesus and because it is an extensive library for the Christian community containing the most detailed accounts of Jewish and Christian conceptions of God spanning thousands of years. It reveals their philosophical and moral insights, religious doctrines, doubts, fears, and questioning, and their sense of justice, pangs of conscience, and struggle to make sense of the world. It must be always kept in mind, however, that these stories and accounts are almost exclusively written from elite male perspectives and are there-fore unfortunately limited. We must pass on the edifying stories, shorn of any bigotry, that still have plenty to teach future generations.

Christians are those who have known divine revelation and enlightenment through reading or hearing the sayings and parables of Jesus, but many have also experienced, in a vision or other mystical event, a direct encounter with God or Jesus as God's incarnation, with the personal receipt of something such as guidance, warning, protec-tion, comfort, or strength from a risen, living Jesus, no longer simply Jesus of Nazareth, teacher and prophet, but Jesus the Christ, the cho-sen or anointed one who still represents God on earth.

We might have experienced the divine in other persons of the past or present or even in angelic visitations, but for the Christian a meeting with Christ remains peculiarly special and permanently captivating. It is this "gift" of the Incarnation, God's presence in (through or with) a human "anointed one" who endured and overcame the worst of wick-edness and pain and then death itself, which allows our finite minds to comprehend and aspire to the true nature of a God who would other-wise remain a mystery, distant, aloof, and—in practice—largely irrel-evant. It allows us to describe our God, movingly and powerfully, in terms of sacrificial love, compassion, justice, peace, forgiveness, and endless creativity. This is what gives the Christian message its enor-mous potential to transform lives for the better.

Mystical encounters with Christ are of course deeply subjective psychological or spiritual experiences colored by the images of Christ that our cultures have exposed us to, ranging from the ambiguously gendered Christ depicted in early church art to the more masculine, bearded figure of imperial and militant Christianity. However, mystical experiences are often a potent source of inspiration and motivation, and thus remain significant alongside (and hopefully influenced by) the revelations of reason, science, and scholarship.

Why Reflection and Meditation?

The liturgies are reflective in content and style in order to establish a pattern of quiet contemplation leading to insight on a deeper level than our day-to-day consciousness allows. Reflection leads to a greater awareness of self and of others, as we really are, and prioritizes shared inquiry over instruction from above. This allows humility, with its slowness to judge and quickness to listen, to take the place of our often judgmental and self-righteousness streams of thought. Reflection reminds us that we are all on a journey of faith and none of us has yet arrived.

This book ends with a chapter entitled "Meditations for Worship and Well-Being." In my experience it is the practice of meditation that is the most valuable foundation for growth and development in faith, worship, and religious practice because it addresses the underlying insecurities many of us have which militate against spiritual progress and a healthy understanding of or relationship with God.

Unless our personal devotions include an increasing insight into the neuroses and superstitions that are the driving force behind much of what we are and do, it is easy to remain in an immature condition in which our lives are held captive to all kinds of dark undercurrents of unreason and fear and in which we never experience the full maturing of our character and faith with all the rewards that can bring. Finding rational explanations dull, people often find the paranormal, the mysterious, and the unknown far more exciting, since they suggest our world is much less prosaic than we might fear. However, such temptations have to be abjured since they lead to a frightening and tortured world, enchanted more by witches and demons than angels and cherubs, such as the one envisioned in medieval times. Meditation releases us from self-deception and the ruse of others to begin a journey toward fulfilling a spiritual potential, not inimical to reality but giving us instead increasing insight into things as they really are behind all the fog of our illusions.

God is unlike us since God exists not just in the dimensions of which we are aware but beyond in the realms that science is only starting to touch upon and beyond even those. It is hard for us to freely relate to God, with our emotions of love, reverence, fear, anger, and so on that depend upon our circumstances, and to address God in prayer as if God were a person like us, without gradually accumulating unhelpful beliefs about God and inconsistent notions about what God is like or ought to be like, born of expectations unfulfilled and mere projections of our own passions and complexes. It is hard but not impossible with the help of meditation and reflective thought.

A Beginning in Healing

The *Liturgy of Healing*, which was the first to be in regular use, has its focus on healing, simply because a church that claims to be founded on the acts and principles of Jesus of Nazareth, if it exists for anything at all, must exist for the healing of the people. It must exist for the restoration of our own and our neighbors' health in body, mind, and emotions, and the restoration of peace and justice in our communities, nations, and world. All of us carry the wounds or scars of past or current sufferings, mistakes, disappointments, and disputes. We require the times and spaces that communities of faith can provide for personal and collective healing and reconciliation. A church is, after all, a body of people who, following in the steps of Jesus, dedicate themselves to sacrificial, costly service for the greater good of individuals, the community, and all of life beyond, opening its doors to the suffering and pain of the whole of creation and bravely taking up the cause of the vulnerable. If it tries to hang on to its life, it will lose it. If it moves confidently into the future, risking everything, it will surely save it.

Who Are They For?

The liturgies are written for congregations which may value the use of liturgy as a new initiative to enhance both worship and theological education. They are also written for congregations more familiar with liturgy but who would like to move away from the traditional wordings to a modern and progressive expression of faith. The latter preserves the essential insights of older traditions while embracing contemporary knowledge and striving to remain informed by front-line scholarship. These liturgies are written, most importantly perhaps, for the many people who can no longer accept outdated and all-too-often chauvinistic assumptions which still underlie or are fundamental to many traditional church services.

There are many dogmas which are no longer credible, given our much more advanced understanding of humanity and our universe. For many twenty-first century people, much of what is written in older liturgies is no longer possible for them to say with sincerity or conviction, but the teachings of Jesus and the Christian life are still profoundly compelling. Perhaps the largest group of people that will benefit from modern liturgies like these are women, since almost exclusively male conceptions of God are evident throughout the Bible, traditional liturgies, and much of Christian history. This subjugation of the feminine originates in the very mundane fact of the disparity in size and physical strength between the sexes and women's further vulnerability with respect to their greater role in carrying and raising children. Consequently women have always suffered a power deficit, and men have rarely resisted the temptation to exploit it.

Thus stereotypes were reinforced down the generations by inflexible dogma and the teachings of men such as the "church fathers" whose understanding of many aspects of reality was severely limited by their time, cultural context, and personal prejudices. Where it was once believed, for example, that women were inferior incubators of man's seed and therefore only carriers rather than creators of the next generation, and that women originated from one of Adam's ribs, we now know that women in fact pass on as much genetic material to further generations as men, and that the first human being was most likely a woman. It was also asserted that just because the Christian incarnation of God happened to be a man, Jesus, that women could not reflect God's image or glory in their bodies. This is just one example of many ignorant and small-minded elements within a theology that sees the human male as the pinnacle of creation.

The grievous treatment of women, half of our human race, which has blighted most of human history, is perhaps the most important example of the harm that flawed and rigid dogma can cause or exacerbate. Throughout our history women have been abused and exploited, censored physically and intellectually, prevented from engaging in public life, barred from education and from developing and demonstrating their talents, and indoctrinated in inferiority from infancy. There, however, have always been a minority of women who have achieved great things despite the odds and adversity they have faced, and we are a young species, so there is much hope for a very different future.

The liturgies in this book use either genderless or gender-inclusive language throughout. It was important to try to achieve a balance when using gender-specific pronouns. Since there is a particular focus in Christianity on a male incarnation of God, and also common masculine terms such as "Lord" and "Father" in Christian prayers, the gender balance is redressed by using the female pronoun for God a little more often than the male and coupling masculine terms where possible with feminine equivalents, such as "mother." The changing attitudes toward women and other groups, especially minorities, have often been a response to new knowledge of science and other disciplines that have had a great bearing on the advance not just of technology but morality and the way we treat one another, often well beyond many people's estimations, just as the insights into the human heart evident in the New Testament were a great moral leap forward from the "eye for an eye" retributive justice of the Old Testament. God is indeed still speaking in ways that may sometimes surprise us, and as much today as ever before.

Modern liturgies are, therefore, greatly liberating, as those who have faith but do not belong to a spiritual community are at last free to become part of one. They are free, without compromising their integrity, to partake in its joys of mutual endeavor, trust, and support, and of friendships based on values deeper than common interest, which bridge many of the social divides that exist in society. New liturgies also allow a fresh exploration of human spirituality and the development of healthy conceptions and experiences of the divine which are accessible to people of all religious backgrounds and none and can wonderfully transform lives.

Our modern understanding, especially of human history, diversity, biology, cosmology, and psychology, have launched all religious people into a new era of faith and practice, and there is ultimately nowhere to hide and no way back for those who are afraid of the future and cling to the past. It is this fear and regression among the religious that has caused vast numbers of people, including a majority of Europeans, to find themselves alienated from religion and the churches. These also include many who claim to be "spiritual but not religious," and even more who would like to have faith and would even prefer the churches to be the heart of their local communities, rather than faceless community centers run by disinterested bureaucrats or disparate clubs and associations, whose memberships reflect only a very limited demographic. If the churches would only catch up with secular knowledge and even with the most sophisticated secular moralities which have in many ways surpassed the moral dictates of the traditional churches, then many would surely return to the increasingly empty pews.

Despite the apparent decline in numbers attending church services, there are many on the fringes who have not yet given up on the idea of church. The liturgies I have written in this book are aimed at kindling that flame of hope for a modern, relevant, and inclusive church that could one day become the heart and soul of society. They are sympathetic to those who have left the church but would consider returning if a radical modernization of its worship and teaching took place. I hope the liturgies will also ignite a passion for pioneering and progressive ministry within those already immersed in the activities of the established churches. When I use the term church, I mean simply a Christian community of faith and have begun, in this preface, by speaking so definitively of church rather than the individual life of faith, because my liturgies explore the social implications of Christian living as much as the merely personal.

The liturgies in this book are written so as to be appropriate for use in progressive and modern-thinking churches of any denomination. Additionally, their egalitarian nature means that they encourage every individual to take responsibility for the direction and future of the church, rather than a select few assigned leaders. I deliberately refrain from using a theologian's jargon, not because I deem my readers insufficiently intelligent to master it, but because the language of academics in their various subject niches often serves only to muddy the waters and would detract from the main aim of this book, which is to assist people in all walks of life to live out and articulate both to themselves and to others a relevant Christian faith.

As important as specialist theologians and ecclesiastical historians are for the church (and I discuss this below), theology has for far too long been the province of elites, and elites that have been very set in their insular and haughty ways. Our human quest to understand God and our faith must now become the project of all.

Practical Advice

These liturgies are written for reflective services which are quieter and take on a gentler pace and more seamless form than traditional services. There is an emphasis on silence as much as on speech or song, giving space and time for thoughts and emotions to run their course, bringing new ideas to our minds, and cultivating a keener awareness. The skillful use of pauses and silences and where they are placed is just as important as how much silence there is overall. The services should flow gracefully and poetically, capturing both the gentleness of the "still small voice of calm" and the drama of the divine narrative on the stage of human history. If a suitable rhythm and atmosphere are maintained, each service outlined in this book will be at least one hour long, though the liturgies that include times for writing prayers, discussion, personal contributions, and special rituals and events such as baptisms may be considerably longer.

These services are especially suited to smaller, more intimate gatherings, where sitting in more inclusive formations such as a circle rather than in rows or pews is possible. This enables each person to have an equal presence and an experience of fellowship with every other in the group. The liturgies are ideal for use in comfortable and familiar environments, for example, when used by home groups, house churches, families, or simply some friends gathered on a hillside or around a fireplace. However, they are equally suited to meetings in churches and chapels where there might be the added benefit of objects and architecture which help create an atmosphere conducive to the elevation of the mind and spirit. The liturgies also achieve a holistic perspective and provide excellent foundations for subsequent business such as the formal gatherings of committees and task groups in the church and elsewhere. It is hoped that these liturgies might also spark a revival of family worship, providing the necessary structure for parents and children to come together to nurture and share in the excitement of one another's spiritual growth.

It is important that different voices are heard during services, and so several voice parts are indicated in the liturgies. These are only suggestions, however, and experimentation is encouraged. The whole group responds in unison wherever the words are written in bold. Those who read the solo parts should be well prepared or experienced in leading worship and speaking publicly so the words are articulated slowly and clearly with the right emphasis and the appropriate use of pauses and silence. Brief explanations are given of elements in the services that might be unfamiliar to participants. When it is indicated that background music should be played, this can be recorded chanting, choral music or live music, but it should of course be contemplative and nonintrusive in volume and tone so that worshipers are not distracted from their personal thoughts and prayers. Instrumental music or singing in a foreign language may be ideal, as words can be distracting unless a song can be found which stimulates thought around the particular theme of the liturgy.

The music for the sung refrains in the liturgies should be either generally known by the group or simple enough to be taught at the start of the service and adapted easily to the size and voice range of the group. It should be progressive and inclusive in its theology and composed in a style that contributes to the meditative atmosphere of a reflective service, characterized by repetition, soothing melodies, and sustained notes to give resonance to the message they carry.

Taizé songs such as "Ubi Caritas," "Deus é Amor," or "The Kingdom of God Is Justice and Peace," and so on, are ideal for the sung refrains and can be easily and beautifully sung a capella (without instrumental backing) if necessary or preferred. Singing in harmony (in parts) should be encouraged and taught wherever possible. It is recommended that the group sing in Latin or alternative modern languages as this not only adds an international dimension and world perspective to the worship, but singing in another language which has slightly different emphasis and different shades of meaning associated with its words can also refresh certain teachings and theology for us—as long as the translation is provided, of course!

The sung refrain in which a few words are repeated is ideal for introducing worship in many languages. The sung refrains at the end of the liturgies can be a repeat of what was sung at the beginning, to highlight the journey of growth, thought, and healing or other transformation that has taken place in between. Each refrain should be sung repeatedly for as long as the particular group wishes to maintain this kind of vocalized meditation, eventually fading to silence and stillness.

In addition to a circular seating formation, it is advisable to have a table display in the center because it provides a comfortable place to rest the eyes and a means of lifting the spirit with beauty, such as a flowering plant or naked flame. The display could alternatively include a sculpture, an icon, or a painting intended to provoke thought or anything else which is relevant to the theme, triggers the imagination, or holds the gaze.

Ideas for these and for participatory activities during the services are given throughout the collection. There are also instructions given within the liturgies for the benefit of those leading and planning the services. I recommend using incense, scented candles, contemplative music and handheld objects with evocative textures to engage more of the senses and add new dimensions to the reflective experience that will make for a total worship involving both body and mind.

I suggest the use of candles in almost all the liturgies because they are easy to use, fairly inexpensive, and already powerful symbols of courage, hope, and solidarity which have been used in historic candlelit vigils and marches, such as at the falling of the Berlin Wall. However, it is important to remember that the aids to worship must be appropriate, not just to the theme but for the particular group of people attending, or they will greatly detract from the value of the service.

Displays should be simple and elegant. Do not be over-ambitious. If something cannot be done well, it should not be done at all, and a simpler option will suffice. Another common mistake is to force activities or images more suitable for a group of children upon teenagers or adults for whom the atmosphere of worship and the raising of aspirations is entirely broken as a consequence. There can be a great deal of woolly or juvenile thinking when it comes to services of an alternative form, and this should be carefully avoided. There are many people who leave the churches because they simply do not know how they can remain Christians in community while preserving their intellectual maturity and integrity. They need a theology, expressed in corporate worship, that is progressive without being vague or confused, and that is neither spinelessly apolitical nor too politically partisan. They need a fair-minded theology with both structure and substance.

These liturgies are written for repeated use, since it is only in their repetition that the meanings of the words and the theology they convey can be explored at deepening levels. Participants can engage with the words in new ways at each hearing, as they come each time with a slightly different perspective. For some worshipers it will be important to read and mull over the content of the liturgies before taking part in a service so that they can take ownership of the words and prepare themselves for a more focused period of contemplation. This is easily arranged for small groups where members are known to the organizers, but for open church services where there will usually be a few worshipers reading the liturgy for the first time, a regular repetition of services is even more crucial.

Do not be concerned if only a few people attend at first. Persevere, because it can take a long time for people to realize the worth of this kind of venture and even longer for them to incorporate it into their busy schedules. Others are used to constant entertainment, distraction, or chatter and may find it takes them some time to learn even to be comfortable with silence and reflection, let alone to reap its many benefits. However, the rewards are well worth the waiting, the frequent reassurance, and the gentle prompting.

The liturgies are written so that they can be used for special occasions such as Christmas, Easter, and Lent, which reflects the importance of the Christian year and the rites of passage in our lives that help to establish a relevant and consistent faith that can stand the test of time and flow with the existing rhythms of our months, years, and habits of memory. The Christian year addresses our psychological need for the stability and order of repeated patterns of practice. The Eucharist or Communion is a focal point for many of the liturgies since it is both an outward and inward act involving all the senses, which is a symbolic and powerful reminder of the core teachings of Christianity.

Sermons do not feature in the liturgies because it is hoped the liturgies will encourage the use of the humble parable in teaching during corporate worship rather than preaching and biblical exposition which can so easily become a means of self-aggrandizement, an outlet for self-righteousness, or a way to limit rather than enhance people's ability to think independently. Public lectures and scholarship are vital and preferable for the education and formation of a healthy Christian community and have for far too long been neglected in favor of the overambitious sermons of preachers who presume to take on the whole teaching responsibility of the church but without the fairness, the rigor, or the accuracy of the specialist. An education that can be provided by lectures and forums for scholarly exchange, alongside carefully thought-out liturgies that provide theological checks and balances and thought-provoking parables that encourage creativity and inquiry, seem a better route to take for the future worship and teaching practice of the church.

The meditations on scripture in the liturgies are a deliberate move away from the disembodied readings (readings out of context) characteristic of many traditional church services. The latter often contain morally offensive passages or chauvinistic undercurrents and yet are still read in a ceremonial way which seems to sanction or justify their contents and imply (whether intentionally or not) that they should be understood as conveying truth in the literal words of God. This is particularly unhelpful in a time when the majority of people no longer have the biblical knowledge to fill in the contextual gaps accurately themselves and gives the modern-minded newcomer a very bad impression of what Christians stand for.

In contrast, the readings contained within the liturgies here are carefully chosen for their clarity, inclusiveness, and relevancy, complementing the rest of the liturgy. The readings chosen do not require an explanation of biblical or historical context to convey their message, because it is clear from their liturgical context that they do not need to be understood in a literal sense. I have used a practice based on *lectio divina* for the meditations on scripture, not because scripture has a magical effect of some kind that distinguishes it from any other writing, but because it is important, even in the light of the best of biblical criticism, to retain the tradition of dwelling intently on the wisdom to be found in such writings.

The Bible still holds a special place in the hearts of most Christians, at the very least in virtue of its long history as the mainstay of the faith alongside church tradition. For this reason, and out of respect for the majority of Christians, the scriptures still demand particular consideration above wider literature. To provide an analogy: as children grow older and begin to see the errors and shortcomings of their parents, they still continue to hold them in special esteem and affection, and the same relationship exists between Christians and the Bible. Such readings are also important in that they continue to tell the stories of our church and community's past, which will always be part of our own history and shared identity.

It is the New Revised Standard Version of the Bible that is used consistently throughout this book because of its scholarly accuracy and gender-inclusive language. As is the case with all church services, enticing refreshments and a chance to introduce people to one another is the best way of welcoming participants either before or after the period of worship. Dry and stale biscuits with stewed tea and instant coffee is always a great disappointment. However "spiritual" people might like to think they are, it is good food, drink, and company (the basic ingredients of good hospitality) as much as religion that will keep them coming and allow the building of community! It is all too easy to scrimp on such things, but this is always a grave mistake. If you are on a tight budget it is still possible to provide simple but delightful hospitality with a bit of forward planning—travelling in the developing world where hospitality is often of the utmost cultural importance, certainly teaches one that!

On another practical note, which pertains to all the liturgies, your denomination may require an ordained person to administer Communion. If you have organized a service inviting members of your church and you do not want to unwittingly break the rules of your church, you should ask an ordained person to clarify the rules and if necessary ask that person to read the appropriate voice part, breaking the bread and distributing it first. You have probably guessed that I would have few qualms about breaking such rules, but I understand that there are circumstances in which doing so may cause an unnecessary obstacle for other worshipers, and it is best in these situations to comply with convention.

ONE

Toward a Positive Future

The liturgies in this book are liturgies of vision and hope for the mission of the church, delineating a way forward. They draw out the essential insights of Christianity, rescuing them from obfuscation, and provide a means for making them widely known. Below I briefly outline the areas of insight that underpin the liturgies that follow and which I believe must come to the fore in the churches' reflective understanding of their mission and purpose. These themes are also aspects of that broader quest for spiritual maturity to which we have been less than fully committed but which must become our priority.

Permanence and Impermanence

An insight common in many religious traditions is that of the transient or fleeting nature of all things and the need to find methods of coping and adjusting, not just physically but socially, psychologically, and spiritually, to the constant movement of a changing reality. The Christian faith, as already mentioned, has shown enormous capacity for evolution and adaptation to new times and environments, and this has been essential for its survival and the survival of its most profound moral and spiritual insights. The latter in turn have enriched that wider context beyond church walls. As a Christian one commits to passing on a faith that transforms people and communities, enabling them to be better and to live better and sending them out on their own journey of faith. One commits to a bold experiment in new ways of expressing and passing on wisdom, trusting God with the results. The church needs to continue in its evolution if it is to survive as a community that provides a spiritual home not just for the elite but for all who come in search of God.

Understanding and coming to terms with the brevity of life and the swiftness of change has been balanced in Christianity by the permanent and benevolent presence or omnipresence of God. The chief concern of this God is not power and judgment and the submission of humanity, or even the overcoming of suffering; it is rather about love—boundless, eternal love, something much more indulgent and much less pious. The Christian life is not only about coping and keeping pace with a changing outer reality or about administering justice; it is about luxuriating in that restorative and munificent presence.

It is also about cultivating a permanent inner character of moral astuteness and loving-kindness in dependence on and in imitation of God's love, which opens up the possibility of a much fuller, more wonderful existence. This balance of the permanent and the impermanent has been a point of perennial contention among Christians, as what is essential to the faith has been so variously defined, itself evolving with the years. However, that central tenet of the faith, that the Christian God is a God primarily of love, is undoubtedly accepted by all expressions of the faith, even those which only accept it in token and have so evidently failed to respond to it and to reflect it in their actions.

Ecumenical and Interfaith Dialogue

The diversity of Christian expressions throughout the religion's history has led to schisms and the emergence of new denominations but also to ecumenical dialogue and reunifications. The churches should therefore be all the more confident about the potential for interfaith dialogue, which is increasingly urgent in our time, particularly between Christians and Muslims, given the growth and political and social influence of Islam and the checkered history between the two faiths. In conversation we are reminded that there is more in common between faiths than we might initially suppose and in some cases more in common across the faith divide than within faiths. A conservative and dogmatic Christianity, for example, has much more in common with its conservative counterpart in Islam than with the liberal wing of its own religion, which of course is ironic given its total rejection of the validity of other faiths. Progressive Christianity, similarly, has much in common with progressive streams in the other religions, but given its inclusive theology it has far more scope for working with them to address the world's problems.

This is one of many reasons why progressive Christians should seek to build such relationships rather than expend precious time and energy on the impossible task of trying to persuade fundamentalists to consider different points of view before they are ready even to hear them out. Some of the older denominations that try to loosely hold together churches representing the full theological spectrum are constantly held back from important work by endlessly having to implement strategies of compromise and appeasement such as commissioning theological talking shops which delay decision making on issues that might prove divisive. These only give more opportunity for repetitive arguments to be had and for resentment to build up and are therefore counterproductive. They also demonstrate to the wider public that the churches are outdated and ineffectual. These institutions will need to negotiate separations, as amicably as possible, so that more positive and productive alliances and collaborations can be sought.

Conceptions of God can be poles apart because they depend upon the way a person interprets his or her scriptures, the authority ascribed to them, and the teaching of his or her local church, mosque, or temple, and these things can vary enormously within the same religion. A sophisticated understanding of scripture and a keen moral sense spans many religious communities just as fundamentalism and moral degeneration does. Having said this, it is interesting to note that the threat of schism within the broadest denominations usually comes over sexual rather than theological issues, revealing that it is not so much theological integrity that is a primary concern to conservative Christians but more carnal matters such as the desire for sexual dominance on the part of men.

Ecumenism within reason, is vital for church progress and growth. Some denominations are close enough in their outlook to forge alliances, especially on particular moral issues, and their combined weight in free speech and at the ballot box can be a powerful force for good. Where these churches differ they may in fact be complementary rather than competing, providing for different worship and practical needs that one organization could not have met so effectively. It is also important to note that the thriving of less dogmatic and more diverse churches does not result in overall decline as is often thought. We only need to look at the resurgence within Buddhism to see that a religion of multiple expressions and, in this case, one which is not even proselytizing can spread rapidly in modern times in both the East and West. It can do this because within its teachings are true observations and insights that will in virtue of their relevance and integrity be sought after and propagated. Truth will always find its way into the open, however much people try to suppress it.

The liturgies in this book provide encouragement for churches to move forward together. However, they do not leave a theological vacuum or hinterland of compromise that would allow conservative elements to hinder the progress that is vital for ministry and mission to all people. Ultimately there are things more important than unity. The overarching sense of the sister/brotherhood of all the followers of the way in all traditions, that can be felt at the best of ecumenical and international events, is preferable to an uneasy formal unity in which everyone is pressured to conform to the edicts and practices of one organized church.

Ecclesiastical unity is to be held as an ultimate goal but not to be sought as a priority in the present time at the expense of our calling to work toward peace, justice, and the protection of the vulnerable. People occasionally have to part ways and mature over time before they are in the right frame of mind to come together again, and when they eventually do, they may be all the stronger in their unity for their period of separation. It is also the case that separation does not necessarily imply ill will. In fact ill will may be lessened as people are set free to focus on positive action rather than ongoing disagreements. Some denominations have competed for adherents, which has obscured the Christian message and brought only the ridicule and scorn of onlookers, but others have lived and worked quietly among different peoples and accelerated the overall growth and enrichment of world Christianity.

Christianity has several important advantages in our present day. It is a young religion in comparison to others such as Hinduism, Buddhism, Taoism, or its parent religion, Judaism, but its ideas have a human past stretching back long before the time of Jesus, giving it both great potential and great richness. Many of our denominations, despite the mutual antagonism lapped up by the press and in spite of the fact that for most of its history Christianity has been the most intolerant of world faiths, are more closely associated now than they have been since the first generations of Christians in the first century Middle East. This should give us greater hope for cooperation in resolving our shared human problems.

Of Heads and Hearts

It is exciting to see dynamic and variegated expressions of Christianity flourishing all over the world, reflecting perhaps a shifting away from the emphasis on creed, and on membership determined by what statements of belief one will assent to. It is as if some of the spirit of the church before Nicaea has returned and religion is becoming much more about faith or a way of life again, rather than about beliefs (though conformity in doctrine and practice began to set in early under apostles such as Paul as is evident in the New Testament epistles). However, this variety has tended in recent times to correspond with the elevation of the heart over the head, apparent in the great flourishing of Pentecostalism and the charismatic churches.

The liturgies in this book, however, respect the utmost importance of keeping your head screwed firmly on, whether you like to dance, clap your hands, and prostrate yourself, or whether you like to sit quietly in silent prayer keeping your emotions to yourself. This is because emotional incontinence and anti-intellectualism are by no means the path to freedom or the antidote to social control and legalism that they might seem to some. On the contrary, shirking one's duty to think leaves a vacuum that allows the opportunist or the socially and politically powerful to manipulate and exploit the majority for their own ends. Their following, a people caught up in an emotional haze, find they have quickly and surreptitiously had an oppressive ideology or creed imposed upon them by their smiling and celebrity-style leadership.

Leadership structures of this kind are notoriously male-dominated and liable to become corrupt since they hold far too great a sway over their congregations. It is actually intellectualism and the careful consideration and constructive criticism, of the theological propositions being made from the pulpit and their likely consequences for individuals' lives, which liberates and allows those expressions of faith to remain varied and dynamic.

Free thought and questioning is the key to developing a broad theology which remains flexible and inclusive and provides checks and balances which safeguard faith communities from incursion by those who would prioritize self-gain. It is the trained and experienced theologian who is able to discern and address subtle changes in teaching that may lead to unhealthy conceptions of God and other distortions of the truth before many adherents have even noticed.

It is important that everyone thinks with both the head and the heart while those with specialist knowledge, such as theologians and ecclesiastical historians, act as an additional resource within the leadership of the local church to inspire and maintain the intellectual vitality of the church, provide accountability for those involved in preaching and teaching, and get involved in adult education initiatives themselves through lectures, journals, Internet forums, and other media. In fact, it is my view that every local church ought where possible to have associated or office-bearing scholars in order to bridge the widening gap between the academy and grass-roots worshiper.

A major difficulty with religion that is based predominantly on emotional experience is that it usually results in the rapid spread of superstitions. Many of these are about the nature of God and God's interaction with humanity, but the most damaging are those that involve the seeing of "devils under doormats," a phenomenon that is very common in certain communities of believers. Every disruption or inconvenience they suffer is seen to be a satanic attack on God's people and work. The end result are churches that focus and speak far more about Satan and demons than about God and spend a great deal of time "praying against" such things and "praying away" territorial demons in various corners of their churches and neighborhoods rather than following the teachings of Jesus.

Some such churches develop particularly damaging obsessions with things such as demonic possessions and exorcisms, and this has led to terrible misunderstandings of mental health conditions, the consequent mistreatment of adults, and the abuse of children. In extreme cases vulnerable adults and children are tortured and killed because they are believed to be possessed. Superstitions like these are used as a tool by those leaders exploiting religion to gain control and power over their flock. Claiming someone is either under attack or possessed by an evil spirit, for example, always implies a person with special authority is required to perform a ritual or prayer to free them from the demons and that conventional medicine and prayer would not be sufficient.

Such people often claim publically that they believe all Christians have equal access to God's power through prayer, while in practice they encourage the tendency among their followers to believe they are needed to perform exorcisms and are quick to promote an image of themselves as people with particular authority. There is often this discrepancy between what theology is expounded from the pulpit or lectern and what happens in practice, so that the more astute among their congregations who are not often or perhaps never exposed directly to the most emotionally charged and manipulative events are not unduly alarmed or moved to take action against them. It is the very young, the vulnerable, the weakened, the sick, and the desperate who fall victim to the worst of these emotional and psychological (and in some cases physical) assaults—the very people the church should be protecting.

The Sublime and the Ridiculous

Jesus taught the importance of inner character over outward behavior because he knew that only a monumental shift in underlying attitudes could precipitate a real lasting change in the way people treated one another. He was clearly unconcerned with outward vices of little significance such a little raucousness at a party, no doubt involving some swearing and drinking too much. He was even happy to provide plenty more alcohol at a wedding where everyone was already drunk—and the best wine at that (John 2:1–11, the wedding at Cana). Jesus was no disapproving Calvinist, pious recluse, or stranger to merrymaking. When churches lose sight of the sociable, entertaining, and relaxed example to be found in Jesus, the Jew who casually picked corn with his disciples on the Sabbath, flouting religious law (Mark 2:23–28), we lose sight of the God of whom he prophesied and taught, and claimed to know intimately.

A full enjoyment of everything the world has to offer, within the moral limits of God's goodness, is the lifeblood of the church. Jesus is, after all, attributed with the words "I have come that they may have life, and have it abundantly" (John 10:10). The *Westminster Shorter Catechism* declares that our "chief end is to glorify God, and enjoy Him forever," and this profoundly cheerful attitude toward the religious life must never be lost. Nor should we allow it to be perverted by those who would try to persuade us that enjoying God is code for some kind of pious mental exercise which demands a denial of physical pleasure and the distractions of the world around us.

Sadly there are people who cannot bear to see happiness in others (perhaps because of a personal lack of it) and who cannot see that humor or laughter can have anything to do with religion. While such people teach that love for a woman or man or child or any other being in creation is a distraction (even idolatry) that gets in the way of a supposed devotion to some abstract idea they call God—a God who apparently severely limits the amount of love in the world—Jesus, in stark contrast, taught that our love for God is in fact the measure of our love for one another. What we do for others, we do for the Lord. In Jesus' equation of love, our love for God is equal to the love we give to our neighbor, so that the more we give to our neighbor the more we give to God (Matt. 22:31–46). An infinite supply of love is available for our channeling so that we can each take part in God's mission to meet the needs of all, including everyone's need to be greatly and deeply loved.

Humor is one of the insights of faith that the church is most in need of reviving. Many think religion is synonymous with seriousness, even disapproval. Humor, however, is one of the best healers and therefore one of the best means for the church to serve the people. It is one of the softest, most pleasurable, and most peaceful of emotions that lightens and lifts the spirit. One does not have to go to a laughing-for-health club to know that laughter does one good on many levels.

There is a need for Christianity to recognize the comedy in creation, the sublime and the ridiculous, the ordered and the incongruous and pick up on the ways it is used to do so through its art and storytelling. Jesus' stories contained a good measure of humor, as he conjured up images of a camel trying to squeeze through the eye of a needle and pictured his followers being sued for their tunics and responding by defiantly handing over their cloaks as well, trusting in God's provision rather than their own acquisitiveness. The very fact he chose to pass on truths by means of imagery and narrative rather than dictate says a lot in itself about Jesus' temperament. It was clearly not that of the fire-and-brimstone preacher. He appreciated the comedy of life on earth and especially our human foibles, in spite of the sufferings of his people and the dangers he faced: a triumph in itself.

Churches must seek to rise above the envy which leads us to a prescribed mediocrity that stands in the way of excellence and the raising of aspirations. They should carefully avoid any bias toward a narrow religious brand that excludes diverse and rich explorations and expressions of the soul, however eccentric they may appear to the majority. For we do not exist primarily to perform "religious" tasks such as evangelism or even social action but are called first and foremost to an enjoyment, indeed a reveling, in God and creation.

We have to achieve a delicate balance between humility and the healthy ambition that achieves greatness. Good-humoredness is a sign of appropriate humility, of seeing ourselves as we really are, not taking ourselves too seriously. It is a sign of self-awareness, understanding that one has one's idiosyncrasies and weaknesses and is liable to make all manner of mistakes and blunders, even the odd howler. It should therefore be a priority in the church to both lift people's eyes and imaginations to the beautiful and sublime while taking plenty of comfort and pleasure in the absurd.

Rediscovering the Bible

The Bible is important because our uniqueness as Christians is found in the particular stories of our communities passed on both orally and in written form down the generations. In recent years we are fortunate to have had a great deal of literature advocating progressive ways of approaching scripture which can help us to understand its true meaning and its right usage in our churches. The birth and rise of Christian fundamentalism in modern times, that line of thought which mistakenly demands that the Bible must be taken literally in order to be taken seriously, has severely impeded the growth of scriptural understanding among young contemporary Christians. It is essential for Christian communities throughout the world to rediscover their place in a continuing conversation about God which has much older, wiser, and broader origins.

There are signs of recovery in progressive movements that embrace a much more nuanced understanding of the Bible. They seek to understand the scriptures in the light of their historical context and the motivations, agendas, and limitations of the authors. They understand that the blind allegiance to right doctrine is inimical to true faith which in its very nature implies a lack of knowledge and certainty. They realize there is no room for God in a community which claims to know the whole truth. Such a community may find itself godless in the deepest sense, since it is in fact convinced not of the righteousness of God but of its own righteousness and that of its creed.

The stories and myths of any religion that reflect the compassionate nature of our God can help people to be better and do better. A great deal of energy is needed to produce wide-ranging resources for the education of congregations, catering to people of different ages and abilities. The authority of the Bible in our religion needs to be reconsidered so that its writings may find their place alongside continuing revelation, including personal and direct revelation through reflection, meditation, or mystical experience, natural revelation through the arts and sciences, and the workings of the Holy Spirit through history and in the many traditions of Christianity and its parent religion, Judaism. We need to be freed to enjoy the Bible as literature. The words of the Bible, after all, particularly in the more poetic translations, have hugely influenced many of the most celebrated authors of the English-speaking world, including of course that most feted of bards, William Shakespeare.

Understanding Our Roots:
A Wealth of History and Tradition

Those of us who call ourselves Christians have a very contrary history. Our predecessors ceaselessly destroyed life in the name of universal peace. They constructed the most thorough and rigid of social and political systems in an effort to build a realm of God not of this world. They developed the arts and the sciences to explore the depths of reality and the soul, constructing grand theories of the universe, yet they obstinately rejected many of the truths their own methods uncovered.

Desiring to satisfy our deepest human needs, they raised up prophets, visionaries, dogmatists, eccentrics, and fanatics, often against themselves, resulting in the repudiation of many sensible people. There are those who like to think they come from different stock and invent lineages of innocence for themselves while blaming other groups or denominations for past evils. They make the claim that such people were not really Christians and that there was some thin unbroken line of "real" Christians existing through history, defined by spurious criteria that turn out to be modern rather than ancient and conveniently reflect the claimants' own denominational and cultural identities.

They cannot with any credibility escape the truth that the historical contrariness of Christianity is not some later distortion but originates in the earliest of Christian teachings, in the changeable mood and mind of the God portrayed in the Old Testament and in the teachings attributed to the founder of our faith, the man who is recorded as saying on the one hand, "Peace I leave with you; my peace I give to you" (John 14:27), and on the other, "Do not think that I have come to bring peace to the earth; I have not come to bring peace but a sword" (Matt. 10:34). Throughout the Bible there are such paradoxes, inconsistencies, and contradictions, no doubt reflecting the differing agendas of the many authors and the particular needs of their own times. It is these aberrations that have given rise to the churches' remarkable variations, adaptability, and endurance. In different hands, the scriptures, because they are believed to originate with God, can be used to justify the righteousness of almost everything, for example, anything from pacifism through just war theory, and all the way to ethnic cleansing and genocide.

Moving away from this reliance on scripture to a religion that learns from hindsight and the wisdom of our Christian forebears but also from the fruits of other intellectual endeavors in the arts and sciences, we can hope to gain more consistency and integrity in our spirituality. We can begin to understand our faith as centering on Jesus' life, teachings, and mission, loosed from the particular theology of the apostle Paul and the Old Testament conception of a God that reflected the narrow interests of one small group of people and the vengeful passions of their primitive times.

There are those who will be quick now to say that it is arrogant to assume that we can take the high moral ground over our ancestors and the scriptures they wrote and that in actual fact we are no different from them, and that the scriptures are as relevant to us today as they were to those they were originally written for. This criticism, however, is very misguided, since there are some ways in which we, at least many of us in today's world, are crucially different. For a start, we have had to rethink revenge and conquest in unprecedented ways since the arrival of the atomic bomb, the demise of empire, the Holocaust, and the carnage of the twentieth century.

We are much more conscious of the lengths to which evil can run in a mechanized age, toward not just the destruction of others but the destruction of our entire species and indeed our planet. We have a much greater awareness of other religions and civilizations and their parallel journeys through history and therefore of that which is common to all humanity in terms of the moral and spiritual, including conceptions of God.

We have knowledge of the extraordinary complexity of the universe and life on earth that has displaced us from the center of our universe and revealed our dependence on the rest of life and our need to sustain it and be a part of it rather than masters over it in order to survive and prosper. We are some of the first generations to have a broad education on a mass scale and one that for many in the free world includes learning the skills of critical thinking as well as rote learning. Among much else, this has given us the powers of hindsight, that great teacher, since we have a much fuller, fairer picture of history than our predecessors, through modern historical and archeological research and access to many more original sources. We have longer, healthier, and more comfortable lives that we consequently value more highly, and are forced to recognize that value and potential in the lives of others since our own happiness depends upon it. We are no longer so preoccupied with death and the afterlife. We can no longer labor under the illusion that we are self-sufficient, knowing that we need one another more than ever before because of globalization and the specialization of all the technologies that support our modern lifestyles. For all these reasons and more, it is entirely reasonable to argue that we are indeed different from most of our predecessors (bar the very enlightened few), not because our consciences are sharper or because we are innately superior in our moral sense, but because we have been forced by our knowledge, experience, and circumstances to begin developing a more sophisticated moral understanding in order to survive and prosper. Of course it is important for me to acknowledge here that there are great swathes of people who have been notably left behind through poverty and the lack of education, or through indoctrination, and the control of information.

There are those even within free societies that have been brainwashed as children and denied opportunities for free and independent thought. However, for those of us who have been able to take advantage of all that our modern world has to offer, especially the wealth of information that was not available to our predecessors, there is little or no excuse left for narrow-mindedness, apart from the temporary malfunctions such as fleeting superstitious thoughts and fears, or moments of resistence to new evidence that darken our minds from time to time; minds that have evolved little since our hunter-gatherer days and are still struggling to adapt to the rapid changes of recent times.

That we have changed in our perspectives since the days in which the scriptures were written and the days of widespread Christian endorsement and collusion with oppressive ruling classes, slavery, racism, colonialism, the oppression of women, and more recently

Nazism and large-scale environmental destruction is not to say that we are not liable to make the mistakes of the past. Indeed we are still making some of them. It is, however, to say that there is at least some hope that eventually we will outgrow these mistakes, even if only because we are better informed of the ways in which these things failed to deliver what even those who wielded power had hoped to gain from them.

There is also the hope that despite the increasing gulf between rich and poor and the fact that real power is still in the hands of the very few, our new networks of information and communication and our interdependence will enable increasing numbers of ordinary people to use their resources as bargaining tools to determine their own futures and begin to enjoy their share in the fruits of modernity. Beyond these, there is also a more audacious hope that people of faith can develop a new kind of theology that will not only respond to the pressures of rapid change and modernization, being forced to abandon the contrariness of old time religion and its blurring of good and evil, but one which will take hold of the moral sophistication gained through recent experience and provide more stable foundations for the future.

An awareness of our roots, and the origins and development of our own Christian beliefs and practices, has been absent or considerably neglected in our churches for some time. However, the importance of learning from our Christian past in order to secure a worthwhile Christian future cannot be overstated, nor can the importance of understanding past mistakes to prevent their reoccurrence or past challenges and how they were overcome so that we might triumph again. The ignorance of history inevitably leads to bad history, that is, a popular but oversimplified history, which is the surest precursor of fanaticism.

Historical scholarship reminds us that our social and political history both influences and is transformed by theology, that we are children of our time and cultures, remaining somewhat dependent on the limited knowledge and experience we have, while also affirming that when we are determined to think independently of the herd and seek progress for ourselves and our communities, we can bring about lasting positive change. There is something to be gleaned from the history of Christianity in all its manifestations, and it makes sense to harvest the best of what was planted by the full spectrum of our predecessors. It is this broad heritage that will provide the building blocks for a Christian future worth having.

Teaching the history of Christianity in the broadest sense gives understanding not only of one religion but of religion in general since there are many parallels between religions, reflecting our common humanity and its understanding of God. It will help significantly in our ecumenical and interfaith endeavors. Not only are we at a new stage in our ethical evolution, but a great chasm of time has elapsed since the last books were added to the Bible. It is not at all surprising that scriptures written so many centuries ago are no longer wholly palatable to most people. It is critical that we learn to balance more diverse forms of revelation as mentioned before, and approach scripture less as an instruction manual and more of a repository of our predecessors' stories and thoughts about God.

This sounds difficult but, I would argue, certainly no more difficult than trying to strictly follow the teachings of a collection of books that are inherently contradictory and which will land us in all kinds of internal and external conflicts when we find them incompatible with our experience of reality! A balance can be achieved in which we maintain both our intellectual integrity and an ardent spirituality, through reflective practices such as prayer and meditation and a commitment to living in community as church.

Our moral sense has evolved with our understanding of ourselves and the universe we are in, in spite and even, as I have explained, because of some terrible regressions in the form of extreme communist and fascist ideologies and dictatorships, where science and technology and theories such as evolution were perverted for evil purposes such as eugenics. Darwin, a kindly man by all accounts, would himself have been horrified by the forms of social Darwinism that came about and especially by the misinterpretation that his theory was entirely about competitiveness and selfishness. His theory was rather about the inevitable survival of those who best adapt to their changing environments, not some great victory of the "fittest," a term we like to define according to whatever our own attributes happen to be.

Our conceptions of God have always been a reflection of ourselves and our moral understanding as it has evolved and regressed and leapt forward again. In the Old Testament we can see it reflected our dual human nature with its capacity for both good and evil, with God showing vengeful, jealous, violent, merciless, and sometimes murderous tendencies as much as compassion, whereas in parts of the New Testament we learn of a God who surpasses these passions and is greatly superior to us in his characteristics of tolerance, forgiveness, and love.

Every generation has reinvented God according to its own culture and understanding. They could not really do anything else. Even the earliest peoples knew how difficult it was even to give a transcendent God a name, let alone describe such an entity. The accounts of God that prevailed usually reflected only the interests of ruling classes and ecclesiastical elites rather than the most morally sophisticated and compassionate individuals in the communities of the past.

There were occasionally remarkable people who were especially enlightened for their time, cropping up in various places around the world, Jesus being among their number. However, even the voice of Jesus was soon obscured by the vision of pharisaic and prejudiced churchmen, including many of the supposed church fathers within the movement he had himself inspired. Voices from the past are a legitimate source of wisdom for us, especially the voices and inspiration of the most enlightened. The other voices can serve to keep alive the lessons of the past so that we do not repeat their mistakes, and their writings should be carefully filtered to separate the gold from the dross.

We must continue steadfastly in a tradition of those who began to have a superior concept of the divine because they sought a God who was beyond the baser human behaviors and desires. We must also allow academic theology and the churches themselves to be reclaimed by the wider communities around them where greater wisdom is often found.

Faith and Science: A Close Partnership

There are those among progressive Christians who make too sharp a distinction between religion (and other arts) and science, saying that the former is solely about a sphere of life dedicated to emotion, subjective meaning, and the building of community while the latter is about another sphere of life dedicated to the gleaning of facts from deductive and inductive reasoning, observation, and theorizing. Atheists often go even further to say that religion and science are inimical. These seemingly unlikely bedfellows, however, can in fact be integrated and found to be mutually reinforcing. Everything can be described both in terms of the physical processes of cause and effect and in terms of meaning and purpose. Even the most mundane of objects, for example, can have great significance beyond the physical, as demonstrated by the use of powerful symbols such as the hammer and sickle, the swastika, the crescent moon, or the cross, which can hold profound and various meanings for different people and can dramatically affect behavior and influence a course of events. Physical processes can also have an impact upon our character, morality, and our experience of life in complex ways. After all, even a bit of fatigue or indigestion can have a significant effect on our attitudes and behaviors.

Physical events can be translated into a corresponding language of meaning and morality in our arts, literature, and religious thought. What seems a routine event to one person may well be a deeply transformative and sacramental event for another; indeed, the whole of life may be expressed as a sacrament: a physical vehicle for spiritual change. This, it should be noted, is not the same as over-spiritualizing, which assumes a constantly interfering supernatural person or agent. I am simply highlighting the unbreakable bond between the physical and spiritual and between the sciences and the arts in human civilization. There are complex interactions between a process being measured, the measuring tool itself, and its impact on the process and the particular kind of brain interpreting the measurements, which makes learning a highly subjective experience for different people even under the same circumstances, and even when there are general trends and similarities fixed by confirmed facts or natural laws. Making a scientific or rational discovery can in certain circumstances be a deeply meaningful and transformative (spiritual) experience, radically altering our perspectives on reality, creating a sense of profound awe and wonder, and forcing us to reflect afresh on our own lives and moral attitudes. Realizing what their discoveries will mean for them and the rest of us more broadly is a key motivation for many of the world's leading scientists.

Few are in the business of obtaining knowledge merely to file it away in some dusty corner of the mind. If we are too quick to separate science and faith we risk draining the former of its excitement, wonder, and indeed its moral reflection, and we risk draining the latter of its reason. We will end up being bored and one-dimensional during the week and believing all kinds of nonsense at the weekend. For this reason religion and science should remain close partners. Religion should attribute meaning to the world, not just in terms of simplistic categories of good and evil, the godly and ungodly, the righteous and unrighteous, but in terms of a sophisticated morality that builds virtuous character for its own sake, expressed and taught in varied and creative ways, that seeks to understand the complexities of human decision making, taking into account our limited cognitive capacities and our particular environments and experiences.

It should help us to both ask and answer difficult questions and to make hard decisions with both confidence and humility. We are unable to accurately predict and calculate, let alone weigh up, the rights and wrongs of the ongoing consequences of our daily actions and decisions. There, however, are certain things and acts that most of us agree are right or wrong regardless of their consequences, perhaps because an embrace or avoidance of them has been crucial for the survival of our species. In these cases, general rules or moral maxims like the Ten Commandments proved the best way of purveying that message down the generations. Despite these rules, however, we are still often caught, as they say, "between a rock and a hard place." It is still sometimes very difficult, for example, to know whether or not it is better to carry out what we would normally think of as an intrinsically wrong act in order to secure particularly good consequences or for the sake of avoiding particularly bad ones that are likely to transpire if we do not carry it out.

Due to all these complexities or "gray areas," the majority of our decisions are actually neutral rather than right or wrong, or good or bad, and it is important that we see them in this way in order to live a healthy life without crippling guilt and constant self-doubt. The best we can do is to cultivate virtues of character and habit over time so that we can trust ourselves to make good or compassionate decisions wherever possible, neutral ones the rest of the time, and bad ones only rarely. Religion, in my view, with its moral and imaginative reflections, can and should help us to do this better in every aspect of life including science, where many ethical problems arise, and science, in turn, with its ever-increasing supply of the facts, should help religion to do this with far greater intelligence. Each should help to shape and reshape the other as they evolve. Religion, after all, provides a framework of moral practice, repetition, and constant reminders, which are often absent from secular disciplines and communities but are necessary given our propensity to forget. Wisdom has to be committed to habit as well as to memory if it is to endure and grow.

Leaving Behind Childish Things

It is time for us to take stock of all the new experiences and information the last hundred or so years have given us and come to terms with the fact that we, and the select few in our particular religious and cultural groupings, can no longer operate with the assumption that we occupy the center of the known universe. We must grow up and conceive of a God for all peoples and, indeed, the whole of the created order. This section looks at the problem of spiritual immaturity in our midst and how to identify it so it can be left behind and avoided in the future.

There have always been those who have tried to prevent others from reaching the spiritual maturity that allows them to have a broader perspective. There have also been those who have avoided spiritual maturity for themselves, for example, the slaves and social subordinates who became too comfortable with their lot and so collaborated with those who sought to perpetuate their ignorance and obsequiousness. In the same way, a minority of women have taken advantage of misogyny to shirk the responsibilities of adulthood and enfranchisement, preferring to remain infantile in their capabilities and emotions, fulfilling the worst of the stereotypes. The journey toward spiritual maturity is certainly not one for either the lazy or the timid. It can be painful and frustrating, as one has to confront the most difficult questions of life and make decisions in spite of many uncertainties.

Spiritual growing pains are compounded for young people in particular, by their need to navigate a way through the emotional turmoil of puberty with all its associated changes in their bodies and brains and the general travails of youth as each tries to establish his or her identity and role in the world. Succeeding in this, however, and taking on the responsibilities of adulthood with both courage and humility brings the greatest freedom and fulfillment that is possible for humankind. It requires the determination to persevere in lifelong learning and an attitude that relishes each stage of a long journey, despite its challenges, and without expecting to arrive at a final destination in this lifetime.

The immature thinking in our midst is most evident among religious fundamentalists and their very close (in theological terms) but slightly less strident cousins the conservative Christians and traditionalists. From here on I use the term fundamentalism to describe the thinking and practices of all those conservative groups with a very dogmatic theology based on old creeds and a literal understanding of scripture, since they share the same outlook in almost all matters of significance—to a far greater degree than they might like to admit.

Fundamentalism unfortunately holds significant sway among youth for the very reason that they are more unsettled and adrift in the seas of change than the rest of us.

Many of them are vulnerable because they are desperately seeking stability and are liable to settle for a merely specious kind. The immature thinking that fundamentalists so zealously defend, however, completely undermines the reconciling message of Christ in the area of relationships, those between men and women, between Christians, between Christians and the rest of society, and between religion and science, spirit and matter. Their views are self-perpetuating and ensnaring, since they play on their converts' fears of death and evil (using the loaded imagery of hell and Satan) to nurture deep suspicions that stifle any thought processes or lines of inquiry that might lead to spiritual maturity.

This kind of desperation to invent and cling to dogma and certainties is common to groups of people within all religious and secular worldviews and arises from their own psychology of insecurity and fear. Such people feel compelled to create a God in the image of man, which they can predict and control like a puppet—it usually is a man, and rarely a pleasant or enlightened man at that. It is these groups which, rather than encouraging children to strive toward adulthood and giving them the tools to cope with real life as it is, make every effort to keep them in a state of unquestioning obedience and intellectual naivety, always on their guard in case some influence from the outside world threatens to shatter their comfortable illusions.

In this section I discuss my own observations of conservative evangelical or fundamentalist communities from nearly a decade of firsthand experience of working with them, and the observations of others who have also been a part of those communities but have, like myself, had other points of reference in the wider world to compare them to. Despite their focus on evangelism, these communities tend to be closed and closely guarded when it comes to their inner circles and leadership, so personal experience is necessary to understand them.

Though it is best to focus on positive ways forward for the mainstream churches ,as I do in the rest of this book, rather than on combating fundamentalism, I do discuss it at some length here because the damage and pain caused to individuals who are at some point caught up in this type of religion cannot be underestimated or taken lightly. It is good to be aware of the teachings and practices of these churches to help prevent our young people in particular from falling into the traps they have set. It is vital that we remain vigilant so that our own churches do not succumb to the spread of fundamentalism.

It is also important that we have a safe and welcoming space in our churches for the healing of those who become disillusioned with fundamentalism or conservative evangelicalism and who are gradually emerging or reemerging into a normal social life and a life without fear and suspicion. Many people do not find such a space and sadly become entirely averse to Christianity, Christians, and church. Unfortunately, some progressive Christians who have not experienced this type of religion fully or for long tend to underestimate the harm it causes to individuals. Most are privileged white heterosexual males who are much less aware of the current effects and more distant from the potential effects of fundamentalism, and are, therefore, not so guarded against it.

They all too easily and mistakenly dismiss the things that many women and other groups have to suffer as rare or trivial. They also forget just how easily such beliefs and practices can escalate toward greater evils and have done so many times in history. They fail to see that there are only very small steps from religious conservatism to fundamentalism and from fundamentalist bigotry to an attack on human rights that leads to violence, terrorism, tyranny, and war, in spite of the examples we have seen in recent times within Islam. This is a good point at which to note that many of the points made in this section are, if not in the specifics, in a general sense applicable to conservative or fundamentalist branches of any religion.

Below is a poem I wrote in 2007 from the perspective of a man taken in by false religion. It illustrates the real suffering it can cause:

COUNTERFEIT

They gorged themselves on ignorance,
When mine lay naked bare
Ecstatic countenances sealed their unchartered hollows.
The sanctuary door flung wide,
Camaraderie with measure plied.

Fleeing from solitary weariness of what is unknown,
From the unwieldy beast Progress,
I became seduced by certainty, in comely form,
Dressed in the old order of domesticity,
Desiring woman's vulnerability.

Thus blinded by the smog of lust,
I followed the man in front.
A seer of our destiny, or a brother in the dark?
Perhaps it was he who lied,
While many whom he led have crumpled, died.

They spoke ceaselessly of God,
An abstracted one from grimmest tale
Who calls his anger just, his every passion pure
And as a man in a wilderness who hates,
He dispenses creatively bitter fates.

The specter of the "touched" ubiquitous.
My soul began to resemble their polished corpse.
Counterfeit piety, demon-spirited religion,
The sole refuge from the dangers of love,
They became my hell above.

But the passing of time saw me again among the living,
Recognizably a man but a wound upon the road,
Scales had fallen in the mill of affection.
And even faith survived, but in a God who courted me,
On the wings of whose spirit, I was carried free.

In my opinion, one of the give-away signs of a fundamentalist church or a church on its way to fundamentalism are devious methods of "evangelism" in the guise of social or other activities. They often involve inappropriate preaching episodes (often inordinately long ones) at holiday weekends, parties, and other gatherings that guests were led to believe would be of a purely social nature, and even at weddings and funerals where they also have a captive audience.

The sermons focus almost exclusively on presenting the hearers with the stark choice either to believe that Jesus is God and the Bible the inerrant word of God and go to heaven, or not to believe and go to hell. They exhibit some of the shallow hospitality and "love-bombing" tactics of cult groups, quickly losing interest in individuals once they have either been sufficiently indoctrinated or have finally rejected their arguments. They are often so immersed in their own subculture and have such a stereotyped view of the "world" outside and its supposedly worldly inhabitants that they mistakenly believe their targets for conversion to be ignorant of their true agenda and lacking in any positive spiritual insight. They are constantly assessing everyone they speak to in order to determine their spiritual status, whether they are Christians or not according to their narrow definitions, and even how Christian they are.

In stark contrast, mature and honest religion is not judgmental and self-righteous in this way but straightforward and totally transparent in all aspects of its organization, teaching, practices, and social life. Its exponents are always sensitive to the wise and insightful perceptions of others, seeing them as equals whoever they may be, and are as keen to learn from them as to share with them their own experience and knowledge.

Honest religion does not result in individuals having separate communities of friends for work and church life and different personas for each, as is common for fundamentalist or conservative Christians, but allows a much healthier, integrated social network and character to develop based on mutual trust and openness.

Many fundamentalist and conservative Christians take pains to formulate long, convoluted, but very implausible arguments (or excuses) for the inconsistencies, factual errors, and morally abhorrent passages in the Bible, strangely deviating from their usual fondness for taking scripture at face value. The irony is that in these cases, the face value explanation that certain passages are factually or morally unsound because the authors themselves were susceptible to error like the rest of us is actually the most plausible by far. They use similarly far-fetched excuses for not obeying literal interpretations of specific rules and regulations in the Bible that are inconvenient to them (especially when they are inconvenient for privileged males; inconveniences for women are generally maintained), thus resulting in extensive picking and choosing, something they so often criticize in liberal Christianity.

Rather than engage in this double-mindedness when considering scripture, it must instead be admitted that the authors' limitations and prejudices are evident in what they wrote. People should have the right to say this and to think this without fear of being rejected or punished by family or community, and without intimidation or the kind of emotional manipulation that uses spiritual threats or curses. They must be given the healing spaces where they can come to terms with an honest reading of scripture, and learn to appreciate scripture again for the important things it really can teach us about the faith of our predecessors and about God.

On the other hand, it is my experience that the liberal Christians are free to integrate their full experience of life and faith and develop the inward through to outward honesty that brings us peace, because they can be as consistent in their approach to scripture as with everything else. They treat all scriptures in the same way, respectfully yet cautiously interpreting them by weighing up as objectively as possible the available evidence from all the sources they have access to. In contrast, the fundamentalist finds him or herself always inconsistent in the approach to scripture, sometimes literal and sometimes not, depending on arbitrary factors, such as the core group's practical convenience and how easy it is to pull out biblical verses and other random facts to support varying social, political, and very often sexual agendas.

They become unhealthily divided in their thinking, ignoring the biblical passages that contradict those passages which seem to support their worldview and harboring a great deal of guilt, anger, and defensiveness as a result. For some this manifests in two personas, for example, in the case of those conservative evangelicals (particularly those who are scientists) who try to straddle the fundamentalist-liberal divide. They are often to be found defending or assuming an allegorical understanding of the creation stories in their professional life or when confronted in person about their work by a hardline fundamentalist but are also to be found tacitly or more explicitly supporting a literal six-day creationism and its fervent exponents at church on a Sunday or when challenged on the subject of their church's teaching by a liberal or atheist.

They want to believe the literal interpretation of Genesis but know too much about science to be able to swallow it entirely. Many evangelical women also find they are divided in their thinking about how to interpret the Bible on the subject of gender because on the one hand they would like a responsible and protective husband which they naively think is more likely if he is given spiritual "headship" over the family, while on the other hand, they want to be respected as an equal in intellectual and spiritual matters. When looked at with any degree of honesty, of course, such a title cannot do anything but undermine equality and mutual respect and a woman's dignity and safety, particularly since the woman already has a power deficit because a man almost always has physical and social advantages (brute strength, size, powerful positions in society and law, and social conventions that favor them) which make equality a challenge even without the addition of pretentious titles.

Many such women (and many men) sadly miss out on the truly wonderful experience of the equal relationships that they are led to believe are impossible. All those with divided thinking suffer a great deal of insecurity and fear as a result of their internal conflicts. They see the world in black and white and are constantly afraid to find themselves on the wrong side. One of the most unpleasant aspects of immature thinking to look out for is the large disparity between the much preached "love" and the genuine practice of love, together with a lack of transparency or sincerity about motivations for helping others. For those who fall for this false love and are later discarded, the experience can be deeply disappointing and distressing, and is a gross betrayal of trust. However, perhaps the most unpleasant aspect of false and damaging religion is the tendency to talk *about* women and groups of people such as those of different religions and sexual orientations rather than actually talking *to* them on equal terms.

Usually there is a glorification of the male over the female and sons over daughters, with an emphasis on male leadership and the stereotyping of women, who are confined to a limited private sphere of life and deemed to be more emotional and less rational than men; this is a great irony considering the extreme emotional states that characterize the leading male preachers and zealots. Women might also be treated as a distraction or temptation away from God, and even thought to be in some way unclean and more sinful than men. They may also be described as closer to nature in a derogatory way based on the belief that Adam sinned by eating the fruit, while Eve only transgressed because a woman, so they claim, relies more on instinct than reason, has a lower spiritual status and therefore less moral responsibility, and is closer to nature's fallen-ness and total depravity.

These appalling arguments, though irrational and totally incompatible with a fundamentalist's own doctrine of sin, are nonetheless perpetuated out of pure misogyny combined with that desperation described above to iron out biblical inconsistencies. Women often find themselves labeled both as more sinful than men and more stupid, all at once. It is because religious dogma and practices have always been used as a means to control, subjugate, and darken the reputation of women, in almost every cultural context, that it is so vitally important that daughters are educated well, can detect the early signs of this exploitation, making them invulnerable to brainwashing, and are equipped alongside their brothers with the tools to fight against it.

One of the most pernicious ideas spread in our time by theological conservatives, of which young women should be made aware, is encapsulated in the common expression, used by many conservatives, that says that men and women are not equal but complementary. This is of course a poorly disguised pronouncement that men are superior to women but that this is somehow okay because men and women are so different that women will always be needed as men's helpers in a very specific (limited) role that men do not have the time to fulfill or consider beneath their dignity (cooking, cleaning, and childcare perhaps)—as Eve was said to be Adam's helper in the book of Genesis. It is the kind of teaching that plays on cultural stereotypes that still abounds, attacking a woman's basic human dignity and undermining her rights and freedoms. It is also based on the complete nonsense of imagined, culturally conditioned, and hugely exaggerated "differences" between the genders.

It has been my experience that male members of theologically conservative congregations tend to be arrogant with an inflated view of their spiritual status and worth. They are often preoccupied with sexual issues, and those who are unmarried are concerned not to get too close to women, believing that they will either be a worldly distraction or that the women will be unable to stop themselves from falling for the men romantically. Apart from the odd show of forced friendliness, these men generally come across as awkward, cold, dismissive, or even hostile toward women (single women in particular), unless a woman is the current object of their designs for marriage.

Even those in relationships and marriages may show a degree of coldness toward their partners as they "hold onto one another lightly" because they see each other as a potential idol. They and their ministers preach a theology that assumes there is a limited supply of love whereby they can very easily love their partners too much and end up putting them before their God, who is constantly jealous for first place in their hearts.

When men go astray and are promiscuous, unfaithful, or dishonest by stringing a woman along, it is the usual pattern that they are quickly exonerated and the women concerned (or women in general) blamed for either being temptresses and too provocatively dressed or, in the case of married couples, blamed for not adequately fulfilling their husband's sexual demands. Far more attention is paid to women's clothing than to men's moral responsibilities. Such, from my experience, are the general patterns of fundamentalist religion of all kinds.

When it comes to the theological direction of the church, those conservative evangelical communities that do not overtly exclude women tend to quietly set up informal theological forums by invitation, inviting only young men, thereby excluding young women without making it obvious or official. They deliberately prevent women from having the same opportunities as men to discuss and develop their theology, thus making it far less likely that young women within their community will show further interest in theology or leadership, or challenge anything that is preached from the pulpit.

Conservative or fundamentalist women often give the impression of bossiness and even aggression, but these are very common side effects of a person being squashed into the tiny mold of the obedient little wife at home, one which their extensive abilities and lively personalities simply do not fit no matter how hard they and their menfolk have tried to make them. Many women are naturally more able and effective in leadership than their husbands, but because they are obliged to be submissive and deferent to them, they cannot help but gradually lose their respect for them, even the respect they might once have had for them simply as individuals, something which they might well have retained, had the relationship been founded on principles of equality.

These things are often quite subtle in conservative evangelicalism, as in the case of the quiet exclusion of women, those without a fundamentalist church (or well-to-do) background, and those of different sexual orientations. However, they are nonetheless wicked, and allowed to run their course lead to appalling mental and emotional suffering and have the potential to lead to more extreme fundamentalism and an increase in criminal acts of violence such as domestic abuse and "gay-bashing." It is vitally important that women and other mistreated groups are helped to break free from their indoctrination and given opportunities to heal and to rebuild their self-esteem in a sympathetic environment. It is important that the demeaning and dehumanizing experiences they have had are voiced, listened to, and understood, rather than downplayed by those who have had the good fortune not to have been subject to them.

Another subtle sign to watch out for is the misuse of praying aloud as a further tool for teaching, disguised criticism, the spread of personal information (gossip), and the use of religious jargon to appear holy or spiritually authoritative. Another is a strong focus on external holiness in terms of restraining from drinking, smoking, swearing, and so on. Sometimes this model of holiness also includes a middle- or upper-class dress sense, a good background and profession, a nice house in a decent area, and a healthy bank balance.

This kind of false holiness, of course, goes entirely against the grain of all Jesus' teachings. People involved in this kind of religion usually have particular loyalties to a specific church or a short list of approved conservative or fundamentalist churches in their area and encourage young people to go to these only. They have a strong presence on university campuses giving the impression to new students that they are the sole face of Christianity. They might not go as far as cult organizations, where members are directly told to either shun their families and to put the church and its leader's opinions first in important decisions such as where they live and who they marry. However, they might well have that effect indirectly as converts are encouraged to spend almost all their time with church members doing church activities and to see their secular families and all those outside as worldly, living in darkness, and not having anything of much good to offer in terms of advice and wisdom.

Many are even persuaded that Christians from most other churches are theologically suspect and encouraged to remain almost exclusively in the company of members of their own congregation. Some members of conservative or fundamentalist churches remain single all their lives, though they would have loved to be married, and have to suffer a great deal of loneliness and unhappiness because of these unfortunate restrictions they have placed on themselves or been indoctrinated with. This is exacerbated if they are not part of the closed inner circles of leaders and their families, and families who have been members for several generations, where there is often a great deal of social engineering in the form of intermarriage in order to ensure and police the beliefs and lifestyle of the next generation.

Two of the most destructive forces within fundamentalism are the misuse of the powerful emotion of guilt and the constant suggestions of hidden meanings behind every event that occurs, however mundane. People become doubtful but are uncomfortable with both staying in and leaving the church, since at every opportunity they are told that every possible exit route will lead them straight to hell. They end up filled with constant guilt regarding their doubts and their increasing awareness of the inconsistencies in fundamentalist teaching. Every detail of life is interpreted as falling either inside or outside the will of God which creates a great deal of confusion and misunderstanding, since a large part of reality is actually morally neutral and indifferent to us.

They anxiously try to work out what decisions God wants them to make, even in regard to the most prosaic of choices, and scrutinize every possible motive they might have. Everything is overanalyzed, overspiritualized, and charged with intense and unpleasant emotions such as guilt and disappointment when unrealistic expectations are not fulfilled. This aspect of fundamentalism can lead to or aggravate mental health problems, as guilt is a very stressful state to be in, in the long-term. Others start to see God as regularly justifying their points of view or actions and develop a number of delusions about themselves and others. The problems described stem from superstitious or overly simplistic teachings in which God or the devil are constantly thought to be interfering in our affairs and making demands: a very unhelpful conception of the personhood of God.

God is seen as involved with every detail of our lives, both willing all that is and yet judging it harshly at the same time. Jesus is seen belittlingly like a buddy or chum who placates this very contrary, unfair, and disagreeable God so that he will be nicer to us. Teenage girls line up at the front of the church singing "Jesus, take me" in rapturous tones as if he were more a lover than the reason for their faith, and everyone forgets that Jesus taught that we should pray, not to him, but to a God above and beyond us, who can be spoken of and prayed to using the personal terms of human language but who does not interfere in all our affairs in a petty manner and who is worthy of reverence, not diminution.

Reverence must be restored and the personhood of God understood in a more subtle way, for though Christians may have had encounters with God or experiences of divinity, whether specifically in terms of the Incarnation or not, and though it is reasonable to address God in prayer as if God were a person like us, it must be understood that these are mere shadows of the full reality of God and God's relationship with us. We are finite beings, and cannot relate to God in any other way than through the concepts, such as personhood, and the languages available to us. However, we must be mindful of our limitations and always strain to see beyond them. The apostle Paul understood this when he wrote: "For now we see in a mirror, dimly, but then we will see face to face. Now I know only in part; then I will know fully, even as I have been fully known (1 Cor. 13:12).

I am conscious of the hatred and hostility that ensues from fundamentalists of all kinds for expounding a progressive theology and for exposing the truth about their religion, but it is far too important that awareness is spread of these issues for the protection of the vulnerable, for those familiar with it to keep quiet out of concern for their own popularity. After all, those who condemn others to hell and eternal punishment condemn themselves to a life of hatred, fear, ignorance, and folly, and ought to be pitied. It is important to remember that the encouragement of others to remain spiritually immature is never about love but always about a lust for power, control, and sexual dominance, even if some of those involved are not fully aware of their own motives and are themselves indoctrinated. Understanding this is important for seeing through the glossy veneer of such religion with its beguiling language and emotive music, its air of social respectability, its well-dressed, articulate, and charismatic preachers, and its semblance of community.

It is not necessary, however, to become depressed by the noisy presence of those with ignorant and narrow views where they are in the minority. Many, even some of the most fanatical, eventually become disillusioned with the teachings that do not make sense and have no relevance in real life in the twenty-first century; they move away to seek healing and a deeper understanding of God. Indeed, the Christian life is a journey filled with personal transformations: our own internal revolutions, enlightenments, and reformations in which we experience painful transitions with the upheaval of all that anchors us, and the bewildering movement of the points of reference by which we navigate the world in which we live.

One must cultivate a quiet acceptance of the continual flow and flux that God has ordained and be content always to keep on learning as new things are revealed. Narrow thinking usually comes to blows with the complexities of reality and (in the free world) the reasonableness of majority culture at some point and eventually dies out or is replaced. However, because of the great dangers of this kind of religion when it becomes widespread, and a majority culture itself, or gains any political power, it is important to limit its influence as far as possible and make efforts in one's own community to help people to mature in faith and become savvy to its deceptions, thus preventing its incursion, and to help individuals to leave behind the childish beliefs, superstitions, emotional attachments, and judgmental attitudes they might have been raised with or learned in the past.

Adult Education

Adult education is the most neglected, yet most effective means of Christian education that allows people to pursue spiritual maturity. It is also the best means of ensuring that children learn about their religion because parents have far more influence over their children than Sunday school teachers or youth workers, not simply because children usually spend much more time with their parents but because children are more likely to aspire to be like their parents or to try to make them proud, naturally seeing them as their chief models for adulthood. Even when the relationship across the generations is fraught, children perennially seek to please their parents, to win their affections and esteem.

Parents are also alone in their position to provide intimate, candid and lifelong guidance and support to the next generation. Many local churches throw all their efforts into youth and children's ministries but they capture the imaginations and hearts of only the smallest number of young people, and even those few usually persist because they have the encouragement of at least one Christian parent. Most children exposed to Christian teaching without parental influence in this regard do not maintain church affiliations in later life.

They do not enter into Christian discipleship and reach spiritual maturity because once they reach their late teens, having outgrown the teaching at their churches which often remains infantile and outdated, they begin understandably to doubt its claims as they are exposed to realities outside the sheltered world of family and local church. They discover these realities do not fit the stereotypes portrayed by those they grew up with and begin their own journey to seek the truth about life and the universe. It is these older children, teenagers, and their parents who are in most need of materials to help them learn about their religion and absorb its wisdom while maintaining intellectual integrity.

One of the best ways to facilitate the maturing of young adults is to recover the lost art of conversation, Christian dialectic, and the enjoyment that can be had in politely debating contentious issues and learning to disagree without animosity and resentment. Another is to face squarely the pertinent issues of our time such as issues of international justice and peace, poverty, human trafficking, environmental destruction, addiction, and widespread emotional and psychological problems. Taking part in working for a good cause develops the maturity that will enable them to excel in any sphere and to work on the front line in peacemaking and securing justice for the vulnerable.

It forces them to work with all kinds of people they would not otherwise have met: people of different backgrounds, opinions, ideologies, religions, personalities, and temperaments. Exposure to complexities like these and the need to make important decisions regardless of uncertainty helps young people to appreciate the many shades of gray in our world and understand that they cannot have the control over life they might have wanted in the past. They learn to cope with that state of affairs and to view things from many different perspectives; thus they develop empathy and compassion for the "other." The measure of a civilized person, and a civilized society, is the extent to which there is respect and care for the more vulnerable citizens: women, the poor, ethnic or religious minorities, the sick and disabled, the destitute, the very young and the very old, the homosexual, bisexual, or transgendered, and those who are in prison.

Though the liturgies in this book will probably appeal to older adults initially, they also provide material suitable for the education and worship of the younger generation of teenagers and young adults, teaching them the basics of the faith. There is still a scarcity of resources that are accessible to youth while also being progressive in theology and not overly simplified to the point where their minds are no longer stretched. I have written these liturgies in a language and style that is straightforward enough to be accessible to younger worshipers but without diminishing the depth and breadth of the content.

The liturgies will teach them about the life and teachings of Jesus and about how to become a disciple and embark on the lifelong journey of faith. They will instill in them the clear message of Good News or Gospel that will embolden and cheer them throughout the years ahead, steadying them in good times and consoling them when times are hard. It is important not to exclude those children from participating in reflective worship who demonstrate the maturity that will allow them to benefit from it and who will not be a disturbance or distraction for the adults. Any children likely to disrupt proceedings, however, ought not to attend until they are older (with the exception of course of children being presented for baptism during such a service).

The religious education of children and youth should be focused not on the attempt to crouch at their level, but on raising them up with new ideas, experiences, and models of adulthood that they can aspire to.

In the case of many adults of all ages there is a great deal of apathy when it comes to Christian education, most likely because of the demands of the workplace and the busyness of people's lives. Many people have considerable amounts of reading and study to do for work or university and little energy left for pondering and reading about Christian theology and history or comparative religion, even though they would probably acknowledge such study to be one of the most valuable investments they could make in life. This is why it is so important to integrate Christian education into the lifestyles and current patterns of work and worship, making them much more effective and transformative, as well as scheduling additional classes and lectures. I hope that writing liturgies for corporate worship services goes some way toward achieving this integration, as they can convey Christian teaching in manageable portions and establish times for disciplined reflection during weekly meetings and on special occasions.

Leading Our Shared Mission

The liturgies in this book outline our common purpose and responsibilities as Christians in today's world. They uncover the true meaning of mission for the universal church. Individual churches, both the buildings and the people gathered in them, should serve as signposts. They should point toward a shared vision of an ideal society, a society characterized by such things as peace, mutuality, compassion, justice, respect, and excellence. Their ministers and other Christian leaders ought to be the devoted guardians of that signpost, its protectors, furnishers, restorers and rebuilders. They are the people who can provide the means, the spaces, and the encouragement for the whole community in their particular locale to move toward its goals of healing, compassion, salvation, friendship, forgiveness, justice, and peace, which are the central components of the Christian faith and of this book.

We know all too well that our churches are not the microcosm of some imagined heaven or restored Eden, though some of them try to strive for such an ideal and usually end up as "holy huddles" as a result, far from their original goal. Instead, as humble signposts, and despite all their faults and failings, most churches are at least continual reminders for the rest of the world, in their worship and spires, of the highest of human ideals that are so often forgotten. These ideals seem unreachable, almost transcendent. They are like our visions of heaven, only momentary glimpses of the uncontainable reality of God. However, the churches have the potential to flesh these out and bring depth and vitality to the best of humanistic notions of goodness which in themselves often lack the weight and authority that history and narrative can give them.

The richness that comes so readily from religious experience, insight, and conviction has still an unrivalled power to motivate people to be better and do better. Secular morality still lacks the consistences of substance, discipline, and endurance that are needed to brave the globalized and pluralistic world we have created without becoming corrupt. It is all too easily abandoned in favor of self-interest and short-term gain. An effective minister does not take the church and privileges such as living in a democracy where there is freedom of lifestyle and worship for granted. She understands the danger and poverty of a churchless society and throws every ounce of energy into alleviating it.

She should seek constantly to create and recover ways of bringing to all people, within and beyond her congregation, inspiring visions and awareness of the practical and political stepping stones that will lead us a little further toward a society that meets the highest of moral ideals. Her main tasks will be to revive the power of story and ritual for continually reminding and enthusing us to pursue our shared purpose, and to facilitate the emotional, relational, psychological, mental, and physical healing that enables the fullest expression of human personality and allows each person to mature in character, virtue, and intellect, and to reach their full potential over the course of a lifetime.

Unlike national or local government, and despite their manifold failings, the churches can achieve this constant creation and recreation of a social vision from their wealth of experience as part of a faith community that has survived over two thousand years of challenges and persecutions, even those that threatened it with extinction, by reinventing itself time and time again. The churches can demonstrate the way of life that leads to the fulfillment of this vision for a better society. Though the churches always pointed to the reality of a loving God, they have often failed to teach and demonstrate that reality, and as with so many things, even when strengths outnumber weaknesses, it is the errors and deficiencies, not to mention the scandals, that prove more memorable.

We might imagine what would be said of the church if as worldwide phenomena it was eventually to die out. Would the eulogies be fairer and more generous than the contemporary reports, as so often happens in the case of individuals? It is likely that many would appreciate for the first time the incomparable extent to which Christian faith and action has inspired individuals and movements that have changed our world for the better, underpinning the struggle for human rights and democracy and the civilizing of cultures and attitudes throughout the world and in international relations.

Most of the great spiritual traditions, including Christianity, acknowledge that the human being and human well-being require a broad or holistic approach. With their subtle stories, sustaining rituals, and inspirational dreams, they can bring order, stability, and meaning to the life of the human psyche in ways that knowledge and reason alone cannot. Religion and the idea or character of God it conveys, however, has the power to bring either integrity or disharmony to the human psyche, having respectively ecstatic or catastrophic effects on well-being. It is, therefore, of the utmost importance that theology and the religious practices and lifestyle it engenders are not left to degenerate or left vulnerable to hijacking by those unscrupulous persons who insist on extreme traditions and assertions of dogma, which are unsustainable, insincere, deeply incoherent, lacking in compassion, and incompatible with an intelligent understanding of reality.

Christian leaders have a particular responsibility for developing, safeguarding, and articulating a clear and mature theology that leads to healing. Christian ministers ought to consider carefully whether they will lead their churches in a way that is radically sacrificial in serving all people, the way of Jesus of Nazareth, risking their own comfort even to the point of death, or whether they will continue to withhold resources in the hope that this will guarantee self-preservation. They must point to an idealistic vision of Platonic perfection while living within a messy Socratic reality with honesty, patience, and imagination.

Ministry is a kind of art. A science of the divine might exist, but one must accept that it has not and might never be fully understood by the human mind. God encompasses our day-to-day experience of reality and yet remains something more than and better than it. As science progresses and more is understood about the physical world, including how religion and spirituality are manifest in the brain, some people's notions of God grow smaller and smaller, confined to a dwindling pool of what is yet to be discovered. However, one can also take the view that the more that is known, the larger God becomes in our vision, since the divine incorporates, albeit mysteriously, all that exists for us to measure with our senses, as well as everything that may exist beyond what can be known by humanity. Interestingly, the discoveries of particle physics seem to suggest and open up ever more possibilities for the existence of even more dimensions of reality that we may or may not eventually understand.

The only thing that is certain about a minister's lot as she goes about her art is that there will always be moments ahead of doubt accompanied by feelings of foolishness. She would do well, in the meantime, to set about rebuilding and repainting her own signpost, small and meager though it might be, with as much enthusiasm as she can muster.

Though I do believe I have something unique to contribute theologically and pastorally in the midst of the plethora of contemporary Christian thought and literature by means of these liturgies, I do not want to give the impression that I believe I have arrived at a complete formula for twenty-first century Christian living and worship. The following quotation from the apostle Paul captures well the spirit in which this book is written:

> Not that I have already obtained this or have already reached the goal; but I press on to make it my own, because Christ Jesus has made me his own. Beloved, I do not consider that I have made it my own; but this one thing I do: forgetting what lies behind and straining forward to what lies ahead, I press

on toward the goal for the prize of the heavenly call of God in Christ Jesus. Let those of us then who are mature be of the same mind; and if you think differently about anything, this too God will reveal to you. Only let us hold fast to what we have attained. (Phil. 3:12–16)

It is important that every progressive Christian take his or her part in the project of developing a viable theology and practice for the future according to what they have attained thus far. Only in this way will we inspire one another to press on to improve ourselves, better our communities, and help to rescue our planet from the brink of destruction.

TWO

Healing

It is my view that healing should be the central concern of religion. Jesus, after all, according to the Gospel accounts, spent most of his time healing bodies, minds, emotions, and relationships. Compassionate healing was integral to the reaping of the human harvest, commonly thought only to be about making disciples:

> Then Jesus went about all the cities and villages, teaching in their synagogues, and proclaiming the good news of the kingdom, and curing every disease and every sickness. When he saw the crowds, he had compassion for them, because they were harassed and helpless, like sheep without a shepherd. Then he said to his disciples, "The harvest is plentiful, but the laborers are few; therefore ask the Lord of the harvest to send out laborers into his harvest." (Matt. 9:35–38)

The Buddha, to give another example, spent his life teaching a philosophy and practices that would help people to break free from suffering. Most suffering, however, is not categorically physical or mental, emotional or relational. Problems generally affect a few if not all of these areas. A fuller, if not total, picture is needed to ensure that people can be helped to find a path to well-being. Health services, whether national or private, simply do not have the resources to provide the holistic attention that many people need. They do not have the times, spaces, and structures that can support an integration of the healing methods that address the different aspects of our lives. Churches, on the other hand, are in an ideal position to do just that. They are, I believe, called to do no less.

One of our most profound insights as Christians is that the need for healing is universal, arising from the recognition of universal suffering and weakness at the deepest level of our being. This is something extensively explored by the diverse traditions of our most devout predecessors, including those early Irish clerics who wrote their detailed penitential works, mystical writers like Spain's St. John of the Cross and St. Teresa of Avila who explored the darkest recesses of the soul, Puritans such as John Owen who wrote about the mortification of a believer's sin, and many more. This liturgy is written therefore to be relevant for everyone, since we all pick up wounds and scars along the road of life. A focus on healing as the central purpose of faith keeps the church true to the Gospel, preventing doctrines and creeds from taking precedence over moral action with its principle of sacrificial love that sums up Jesus' ministry. It acknowledges the tragedy in human lives while remaining stubbornly filled with hope and confidence for overcoming the challenges that come our way.

The *Liturgy of Healing* also provides a means of fostering more enlightened attitudes to suffering and ill health in general, which ties in with the meditations at the back of this book. While a large part of the healing of bodies should rightly be left to the medical professions, there is scope for local churches to provide leadership and example in promoting healthier lifestyles. This is especially true when widespread health problems, such as obesity, binge drinking, stress, and depression are so inextricably bound up with culture, relationships, and emotional health. It is these complex issues especially which the churches could help significantly to alleviate by providing a supportive community, counseling, mediation and practical advice, and by reinforcing a healthy, realistic perspective on life through its teaching, giving people the tools, such as meditation, to address their problems.

The church should be at the forefront of tackling any suffering that is widespread in our societies. Since a local church cannot of course provide every service required by its parishioners or persons who come in search of help, it should endeavor to be a hub of information about charities and other resources that are available, throwing the net wide with its contacts and research, so that it can refer people to those with the specific expertise to help them. It should be a resource with an outreach to the poor and those who are marginalized or new to a community, who do not know where they can obtain information.

If a church does not assist people with practical difficulties and is only a talking shop, it will not last for very long.

The churches ought also to be at the vanguard of a movement which fully rejects the stigma surrounding mental and emotional illness. Many of the most admirable people who have contributed most to public life have suffered from these illnesses. Those who have experienced mental illness are often all the more insightful, perceptive, and compassionate because of it, and are the very people in society who are driven to make a positive difference in the lives of others. Yet, even today, many sufferers are still looked upon as burdensome and an embarrassment for society and church.

This is a particularly sad situation considering most ordinary people will themselves suffer with common conditions such as depression and anxiety disorders at some stage in their lives. These illnesses are indeed so common as to be entirely normal human responses to the stresses and sorrows that life throws at us. They should not, therefore, be viewed with fear, suspicion, or condescension, but met with warmth, comfort, kindness, and the reassurance that recovery is possible. Though it is impossible to know what such suffering is until one experiences it for oneself, it is important that everyone be equipped with enough information to dispel the myths and misconceptions surrounding mental illness and encouraged to learn how to support people in coping better with their symptoms and in moving through the stages of recovery.

In spite of the stigma, mental illnesses have much better prognoses than many other illnesses, and most people recover and go on to lead normal lives. Ministers and congregations should be educated much more thoroughly in this area in particular, since it is often churches that perpetuate presumptuous, pernicious, and destructive ideas—for example, that these illnesses are a punishment from God for some misdeed, the result of a lack of faith, or the attack of the devil or even possession by an evil spirit. There are also many so-called faith healers who take advantage of desperate people for their own ends. In addition to the ignorance of some religious communities, even the medical professionals to whom they must defer very often have surprisingly little knowledge and understanding when it comes to the area of mental health when compared to other areas of medicine.

They struggle as much as the rest of us to understand the complex interactions of people's experiences, habits, beliefs, emotions, and brain chemistry. Most acknowledge that prescription drugs are not a cure, because they do not address all the underlying causes and only help to alleviate symptoms by altering brain chemistry in ways that are not guaranteed to be entirely harmless. Many doctors are increasingly turning to meditation and cognitive behavioral therapies for more successful ways to treat patients in the long term. Sufferers need patient support, love and acceptance, practical advice or assistance, a stable environment, reassurance, and positivity. These are all things that the local churches could provide.

With regard to the healing of emotions, it is important that emotions are given space and time for expression and that the churches become places where this is possible. Emotions often lag behind our rational thought processes and need time to be processed in our bodies (where we often feel our most powerful emotions as physical aches and pains) and by our subconscious minds until they are eventually diffused. People need to be heard and valued as they are, in the state that they are in, in a nonjudgmental environment where they can be free to express themselves without being stereotyped and where they can be sure of confidentiality.

We live in a society in which people are branded very quickly in terms of their past deeds or misdeeds, their qualifications or lack of them, or according to their past displays of strength or weakness. Intimate details of people's private lives are routinely and crudely exposed. One way in which the churches must be countercultural is surely in forgiving and forgetting people's pasts, allowing them to make a new start and using proper discretion as to what information it is necessary to disclose and to whom. Obviously there are some cases where past actions still have a bearing on the present, for example, when they involved criminality or significant harm to others, and in these cases there might be very good reason for caution or disclosure.

In the case of emotional turmoil, meltdowns, and breakdown, however, it is vital that the church become a place that accepts such things as part of the course of life and does not treat such people differently, thereby deterring others from seeking the help they need to recover. Intense emotions that are too long withheld can themselves lead to mental exhaustion and illness. The *Liturgy of Healing* hopes to encourage a healthy attitude and respect for emotional healing alongside and equal in importance to the other aspects of healing.

The *Liturgy of Healing* is also concerned with the healing of relationships, since dysfunctional relationships within families, communities, and workplaces often underlie or contribute to emotional, physical, and mental ill health. The Christian church has always held forgiveness and reconciliation to be at the very heart of a life of faith and these are the means by which relationships can be restored. They are in fact the keys for unlocking the gates of heaven and bringing about peace among peoples. Learning to live in community, where one has to practice forgiveness and reconciliation on a daily basis, rather than merely preaching it, is essential for building enjoyable and productive relationships and allowing one another the space to heal in any other way that they may need.

An emphasis on the healing of the earth in this liturgy acknowledges our dependence on the rest of creation and its dependence in turn on our actions or inaction. It reminds us of our need for sustainable resources and energy, and the conservation of essential ecosystems, which can only be achieved if we care enough about ourselves, other creatures, and the generations still to come to make the necessary changes to our lifestyles. The phenomenal motivation that will be required to unite humanity in solving the environmental problems we have mostly brought upon ourselves can only arise through a much deeper connection of our minds, emotions, and spirits with the natural world.

If we pursue this fuller appreciation the world of which we are only a part, the healing of our own souls, that is, achieving a sense of wellbeing at the deepest subconscious and spiritual levels, may well just happen along the way. It is because most of us live in cities now that our thoughts have become so detached from the environmental processes that sustain us, while our bodies remain as dependent on these things as they ever were. This is why it is so important to support initiatives that bring nature into the metropolis as much as possible, such as parks, gardens, native reserves with educational exhibitions, and so

on, and to increase the exposure of our children to the natural world
in ways that will instill in them a respect and love for the intelligence,
and freedom, of the rest of life on this planet.

THE LITURGY OF HEALING

> If you know someone in need of prayer for healing and you would
> like that person to be mentioned during the service, you are invited
> to give that person's name to one of the leaders before the service
> starts.

Sung Refrain

Welcome

VOICE 1:
Stretch out your hand, O God,
And write in the sands of our hearts
So that we might not condemn, but love,
So that we might walk away from evil
To a place of integrity and wholeness.
You come among us and share our life.

All:
And you welcome us among you,
God of the heavens,
God Incarnate,
And Spirit of Pentecost,
To share forever in yours.

Still-Speaking Parable:
The Pilgrim

VOICE 2:
There once was a woman who set out on a long pilgrimage. The journey, which took her on foot through a wild and beautiful landscape,
would surely inspire a parallel journey of faith, enriching her life

> The Still-Speaking Parable is a means of storytelling that conveys moral and spiritual truths continuing in the tradition of the story-telling of Jesus. It celebrates the continuing revelation of God to us today and into the future, and demonstrates that God did not stop speaking when the last words of the Bible were written all those centuries ago, nor does God only speak through church leaders and the ordained.

for years to come. She carried a large cross upon which she cast all her sufferings, past and present, and all the deeds of which she was ashamed. The pilgrim resolved to plant the cross at her journey's end and walk home unburdened, delighting in a new lightness of both foot and heart.

As the path wore on into the sunset, the cross grew heavy upon her shoulders. Glancing around in distress, she was surprised to see two distant figures rounding a bend. Catching up with her, they took an interest in the cross and asked if they could cast their guilt and pain upon it too and share the load the rest of the way.

Suddenly it dawned on the pilgrim that she had been living with the assumption that she alone had to shoulder the responsibility for her misdeeds and that her suffering could be borne by her alone, that she alone could put her life to rights. The pilgrim realized she had been mistaken. As her eyes were opened, she saw that in both sin and suffering we are not just alike but inextricably bound together, since in a myriad of ways and with every passing second we influence one another's lives for both good and ill.

The pilgrim understood that to find true freedom from the web of life's sorrows, we must meet each other along the road, hammer our crosses together, carry them together, plant them on a hillside together as a lasting sign, and walk away as one.

Prayers of Occasion

Voice 1:
As Simon of Cyrene helped Jesus to carry the cross to Golgotha,
Let us help one another to carry the cross of our times

So that we might not buckle under the weight of it
But learn to enjoy the lighter load of a shared life
To which we are called, in God.

We unite in repentance from sin;
We unite in the forgiveness of others and ourselves;
The remedy for bitterness and regret.
We seek to unlearn
Our mistaken ways of thinking about God
And embrace instead God's true nature
Of compassion and love.

VOICE 3:
Let us pray for one another:

Pause

VOICE 3:
For those who long for the healing of their bodies

We pray for the restoration of health and freedom from pain.

VOICE 1:
For those who long for the healing of their thoughts and emotions

We pray for the restoration of peaceful minds and hearts.

VOICE 3:
For those who long for the healing of their relationships

We pray for the restoration of love through forgiveness and
reconciliation.

VOICE 1:
For those who long for the healing of the earth

We pray for the restoration of our environment through the
combined effort of all its peoples

Voice 3:
For those broken by trauma, oppression, abuse, and slavery

We pray for their emancipation and the restoration of their
dignity and human rights so that they may begin to heal.

VOICE 3:

For those hurt and damaged by religion and the church

We pray that they will know the love of God and find it in others.

VOICE 3:

For those consumed by poverty and hunger

May we help to bring out of squalor
Those who have yet to see
A place where holiness and healthiness walk hand in hand.

VOICE 1:

We pray for the continued advance of modern medicine
For greater understanding of the human body, mind, and emotions
So that the quality of our lives may continue to improve,
So that there will be less pain and suffering in the world,
So that we might worship with greater joy and strength.
We pray for love and tenderness in the treatment of the sick
That we will have greater empathy and concern for one another,
That no one will be left vulnerable, alone or in distress,
That all those who suffer would not despair, but hold on to you
Until the time of darkness has passed.
May they find peace in God and kindness in their neighbors.
May they find renewal in their bodies and refreshment for their souls.

VOICE 3:

We bring before God
Those known to us who are unwell or experiencing difficulties
at this time, including. . . .

> [*Names collected at the start of the service*]

We pray for those in pain,
For the lonely, the confused, the anxious, and the sorrowful.
We remember them in the quietness of our hearts
And pray for the healing of their bodies
And the comfort of their souls.

May family, friends, church, and health professionals
Rally around them
With sensitivity and compassion,
With expertise and love.

Pause

VOICE 1:
For those who long for the healing of their bodies

We pray for the restoration of health and freedom from pain.

VOICE 3:
For those who long for the healing of their thoughts and emotions

We pray for the restoration of peaceful minds and hearts.

VOICE 1:
For those who long for the healing of their relationships

**We pray for the restoration of love through forgiveness and
reconciliation.**

VOICE 3:
As those who long for the healing of the earth

**We pray for the restoration of our environment through the
combined effort of all its peoples.**

VOICE 1:
For those broken by trauma, oppression, abuse, and slavery

**We pray for their emancipation and the restoration of their
dignity and human rights so that they may also begin to heal.**

VOICE 3:
For those hurt and damaged by religion and the church

**We pray that they will know the love of God and find it
in others.**

VOICE 1:
For those consumed by poverty and hunger

May we help to bring out of squalor
Those who have yet to see
A place where holiness and healthiness walk hand in hand.

Voice 3:
Our God, make us a people who demonstrate love and hope
Wherever you may lead us.
Keep us on the narrow path between harmful extremes.
Take away the fear that closes our minds to the truth,
The fear that causes us to exclude others and seek control,
The fear that causes us to create a God in the image of ourselves,
The fear that places a period where you have placed only a comma
And sees an ending where there is really a beginning.
Take away the fears which keep us from the future,
Because that future is yours and you are good.

Make us a people through whom you continue to speak,
A journeying people who know they have not yet arrived,
A people seeking knowledge and transformation.

Voice 1:
We join together in hope for a world infused by the spirit of God:

Our father in heaven,
Holy is your name.
Your kingdom come.
Your will be done
On earth as it is in heaven.
Give us this day
Our daily bread,
And forgive us our debts
As we forgive our debtors.
Lead us not into temptation
But deliver us from evil,
For yours is the kingdom,
The power and the glory,
Now and forever.
Amen.

Meditation on Scripture

Here a relevant passage from scripture is read several times, slowly and with expression. I recommend that pauses and emphasis be placed on different words during each reading. Different translations can be used for each reading to expose new shades of meaning as long as inclusive language is maintained. For a longer passage, one reading may be sufficient. Through these meditations we pass on the stories and moral messages of the forerunners of our faith.

VOICE 4:

The Man Born Blind, John 9:1–7

As he walked along, [Jesus] saw a man blind from birth. His disciples asked him, "Rabbi, who sinned, this man or his parents, that he was born blind?" Jesus answered, "Neither this man nor his parents sinned; he was born blind so that God's works might be revealed in him. We must work the works of him who sent me while it is day; night is coming when no one can work. As long as I am in the world, I am the light of the world." When he had said this, he spat on the ground and made mud with the saliva and spread the mud on the man's eyes, saying to him, "Go, wash in the pool of Siloam" (which means Sent). Then he went and washed and came back able to see.

Invitation

VOICE 2:
Merciful God, take us and heal us.

Find in me that place of pain
Where peace may make its home again
Take my tender heart and soul
And make it with your love unfurl.

While music is playing, you are invited to go forward and light a candle as a symbol of prayer, bringing before God either yourself or someone you know.

Bible texts for use in the Meditations on Scripture include: Matthew 6:25–34 (Do not worry), Matthew 5:1–10 (The beatitudes), Mark 2:1–12 or Matthew 9:2–8 (Jesus heals a paralytic), Matthew 9:18–26 or Luke 8:40–56 (A girl restored to life and a woman healed), Matthew 9:35–38 (The harvest is great, the laborers few) and Luke 14:1–6 (Jesus heals the man with dropsy). Individual verses or much shorter passages can also be used as a group with pauses in between, verses such as Matthew 11:28–30 (Come to me, all you that are weary) and Luke 12:32–34 (Do not be afraid, little flock) and Zephaniah 3:17 (The Lord your God is with you).

Communion

VOICE 1:
Jesus willingly died because of things done that were evil
And because of things that were not done that are good.
But Jesus triumphed over pain and death
When out of the darkness came the light of the world,
The light of a life that shines still in the hearts of many,
That brings hope to every corner of the earth.
Though Jesus bore the worst of evil and suffering,
He revealed the heights of divine love
And the depths of forgiveness that can be found in God.
He demonstrated in human flesh
Our capacity to manifest this love and grace
And taught us the most excellent way to live.
His message is the good news of what God is really like,
News that does not weigh down the soul
Like the teachings of Pharisees and hypocrites,
But news that lightens the spirit
And brings down the barriers that distance us from God.

We turn away from our wrongdoing
In thought, word, and deed
And from our failure to act for the good.
We seek instead to walk in the way of Christ,

The anointed one,
Filled with divine love and grace,
Telling of the good news revealed in him:
That you our God carry away our guilt
And set us free.
Give us compassion in our turn
To free those who have caused us harm
From our anger and bitterness
So that in a world of conflict
We might be those who strive for peace.

VOICE 3:
 In Christ a new covenant was declared,
Renewing the commitment made in the beginning
Between humanity and their God.

We joyfully affirm the renewed bond of love.

VOICE 3:
I invoke the Holy Spirit!
Come upon these elements in grace and power!
Make this physical act a vehicle for our spiritual transformation!

We invoke the spirit of God upon our family and table.

VOICE 1:
On the night that Jesus was betrayed, he took bread and gave thanks to God. Sharing the bread with his disciples, he said, "Take and eat, this is my body given for you: Do this in remembrance of me."

VOICE 1:
After supper, he took the cup and again gave thanks to God. He said to his disciples, "Drink this, all of you: this is my blood, the blood of the new covenant, shed for you and for many, for the forgiveness of sins. Do this in remembrance of me."

The bread is broken and distributed with the words:

The body of Christ, broken for you.

The wine is shared and also passed around the group with the words:

The blood of Christ, shed for you.

A time of silence is kept.

VOICE 1:
The blood of Christ was shed and his body broken
Bringing us near to the God from whom we had wandered.
And so it was that God intended a family table,
A meal of bread and wine,
To be the lasting sign of a partnership
Between God and humankind.

**We are invited to take our place as sisters and brothers,
Children of a God who is mother and father to all creation.**

VOICE 3:
In this act of remembrance, Jesus taught humanity
How to share all that is material and spiritual,
How to live together in peace and to act justly,
Yet still we fail to distribute our resources fairly
And wage wars due to greed rather than need.
Jesus taught us to give each one a place and voice,
And yet there are those
Who are unheard in conversation at the table,
And many who are still denied their seat.
We pray that God will breathe life
Into our practice of Communion,
That its principles of justice and equality
May become a reality in the world
Around the family tables in our homes,
At the conference tables where we sit down with our colleagues,
At the tables of trade and commerce,
And those around which the world's leaders meet on our behalf.

**Help us to remember you, O God,
Not only when we are alone
But when we are together
That we may always treat others
As we would wish to be treated ourselves.**

Invitation

If you would like, please come forward to be anointed with oil, and the leaders and congregation will pray for you during the silence. This anointing is simply an outward demonstration of our inner prayers for your health, comfort, peace, and renewal. You do not have to have a specific problem or illness to take part. We all carry wounds and scars that are in need of healing.

> At the anointing, the leader can draw a cross of oil either on the forehead or palm of the participants who come forward and can use words such as "May God bless you and keep you" or "The peace of God be with you always" for each anointing.

VOICE 1:
We pray for the coming of God.

Transform our suffering into wisdom and compassion.

VOICE 1:
May our prayers be generous and sincere.

Help us to pray for those we love and those we find difficult to love.

VOICE 1:
We pray for the will of God to be revealed.

Break into our lives like a dawning, and light up the way ahead.

Final Prayer and Blessing

VOICE 3:
Give us, O God of countless wonders,
Ears to hear your words of comfort, and
In times of want and times of plenty
The confidence within that brings contentment
And quiets the voices of dread and despair.

Direct our lives so that they might be an offering
Pleasing to both God and humankind,
Drawing in the lost and the lonely
That every soul may find its rest in you.

VOICE 1:
We who were born in the loving arms of God
Shall one day die into those same loving arms.
Therefore, we are called to serve to the point of sacrifice
In this brief moment in our universe of time and space
Following the example of Jesus Christ set before us,
Knowing that we need fear neither life nor death,

For we are present with God in eternity
And belong to what is more than
And better than what we know.
So we trust each one to your loving watch and care
And commit all our prayers to you
In the power of resurrection hope.

Sung Refrain

THREE

Compassion

While healing is the process that should define our journey through life as Christians, compassion is the method by which it is achieved— compassion toward others and also toward ourselves. Mutuality, facilitated by language that is unique to our species, is humankind's greatest strength, allowing us to cooperate and organize ourselves in ways that lead to our flourishing and our rapid advancement in terms of obtaining knowledge and productive capability. The alternative is unbridled competition and a self-indulgence at the expense of others that leads only to a decadent and dissolute society, and ultimately to the downfall of our civilizations.

The *Liturgy of Compassion* articulates and develops a theology of compassion which should permeate every aspect of our lives. Compassion is neither a cheap sentiment nor a token act of charity; it is modeled on the costly grace of Christ and is the most profound experience of sharing in the sorrows and perceiving the needs of others, combined with the motivation and determination to alleviate those sorrows and address these needs. The importance of empathy and understanding, to some extent feeling the suffering that is common to all creatures, and the importance of understanding that sin, choosing to do that which one knows to be selfish, harmful, or even wicked, is a weakness common to all of humanity: these are key insights at the heart of the Christian tradition which help us to live more cooperative and compassionate lives.

Jesus chose to spend his time with tax collectors and sinners. His was a religion of radical compassion, not one of piety. I prefer to use the word "compassion" here rather than "love" because "compassion" still has in common parlance the active connotations of the older word for love, "charity," whereas the word "love" in recent times has become too closely associated with that shallow and fickle state of infatuation

that flares up briefly between Hollywood's male and female protago-
nists. Love has also become a trite and sentimental notion in some
church circles because of its overuse, especially when in the context
of a vague insubstantial theology. In other church circles it has been
regularly misused, spoken of frequently but like some abstract idea
that exists only in the mind, has rarely had any impact on the way
the members of the community treat one another or those outside.
In fact there are many who have found, just as Jesus did, more real
love among the disreputable than in temples or churches. Night clubs
and bars may leave one empty and cold at the end of the night but at
least they never promised much. Churches, on the other hand, can be
like a mirage, bitterly disappointing. It is important to restore the true
meaning of the word love, and for now this is perhaps best done by
speaking of love as compassion.

Compassion goes much further than contemporary ideas of love
because it is as much to do with justice as it is to do with fellow feeling. It gets right to the core of the Gospel of Jesus. Rather than echoing
all the cataclysmic prophecies that abounded in his day and the Jewish
hopes for liberation by means of armies of angels and other such violent interventions from above, Jesus chose to go against the mainstream
and become himself the prophetic liberator, the one who would gather
the people so that they, rather than angels, could bring about justice
on earth by peaceful means. This was a message of good news because
it was about empowering the powerless, a way for real people to take
decisive action to help themselves in spite of their disadvantaged position in society. It had the potential to transform the world if it attracted
a great enough number of disciples. He took a religious text to support
his cause from a passage of scripture familiar to the people that he knew
would inspire them, words from Isaiah that could be recognized easily
and recited by his followers in full:

"The Spirit of the Lord is upon me,
  because he has anointed me
    to bring good news to the poor.

He has sent me to proclaim release to the captives
   and recovery of sight to the blind,
     to let the oppressed go free,
to proclaim the year of the Lord's favor" (Luke 4:18–19).

The Good News of Deliverance (Isaiah 61)

The spirit of the Lord God is upon me,
   because the Lord has anointed me;
he has sent me to bring good news to the oppressed,
   to bind up the brokenhearted,
to proclaim liberty to the captives,
   and release to the prisoners;
to proclaim the year of the Lord's favor,
   and the day of vengeance of our God;
   to comfort all who mourn;
to provide for those who mourn in Zion—
   to give them a garland instead of ashes,
the oil of gladness instead of mourning,
   the mantle of praise instead of a faint spirit.
They will be called oaks of righteousness,
   the planting of the Lord, to display his glory.
They shall build up the ancient ruins,
   they shall raise up the former devastations;
they shall repair the ruined cities,
   the devastations of many generations.

For I the Lord love justice,
   I hate robbery and wrongdoing;
I will faithfully give them their recompense,
   and I will make an everlasting covenant with them.
Their descendants shall be known among the nations,
   and their offspring among the peoples;
all who see them shall acknowledge
   that they are a people whom the Lord has blessed.
I will greatly rejoice in the Lord,
   my whole being shall exult in my God;

for he has clothed me with the garments of salvation,
    he has covered me with the robe of righteousness,
as a bridegroom decks himself with a garland,
    and as a bride adorns herself with her jewels.
For as the earth brings forth its shoots,
    and as a garden causes what is sown in it to spring up,
so the Lord God will cause righteousness and praise
    to spring up before all the nations.

These words about social justice and fairness represent the message of Jesus more accurately than any messages to do with liberating individuals from the bondage of sin, despite the latter's dominance in the Christian tradition since Jesus' day. I have quoted them almost in full as they are the heart of the mission of Jesus and should have been the foundation of the Christian faith. Sadly, not many of us will recognize this Gospel. This is because the faith that we have inherited has for so long and so successfully obscured and overlaid the message of Jesus with a theology that initially came from the mixture of prevailing Greek, Roman, and mystical ideas which influenced the apostle Paul and other early church leaders. This Gospel was then itself manipulated and augmented ever since according to the interests and prejudices of successive ruling elite cultures.

It is important that through a renewed emphasis on compassion Christians can reignite a passion for Jesus' message of liberation and good news for the poor and oppressed peoples of our modern world, empowering them to engage in nonviolent resistance to secure their own freedoms and human rights. Followers of Jesus are those who would stand in the esteemed tradition of political and social movements based on a sophisticated ethic of compassion, liberty, and equality, such as the American civil rights movement, Gandhi's struggle for Indian independence, and the feminist movement. Though none of these movements or their leaders were beyond criticism, including Jesus, no doubt, they were certainly inspired by a God of compassion and justice, truth, and love, whose transcendence was acknowledged but whose spirit worked within them.

THE LITURGY OF COMPASSION

Sung Refrain

Welcome

VOICE 1:
Hear the call to a life of compassion,
A life neither foolish nor dull,

All:
For bathed in divine grace
And in spite of our weakness
We embark on adventures
Unmatched.

VOICE 2:
Hear the call to a life of compassion,
A life neither foolish nor dull,

For imbued with divine spirit
We find our souls replete
And know no greater purpose
Than to love.

Declaration of Compassion

VOICE 1:
We meet as disciples
Of the God of compassion,
That principle within faiths
Young and old,
Sometimes buried,
Sometimes a beacon of hope,
That we must do unto others
As we would have them do unto us.
For the seeds of compassion
Contain power indescribable,
Transforming the present
And brightening the future for all.

In compassion we are dethroned
From the center of our universe
So another can be crowned in our place.
In compassion we transcend the self
With constant effort and resolve,
Spanning the boundaries between us
And breaking down barriers of politics,
Ideology, tradition, and creed.

VOICE 2:
Compassion springs from mutual dependence,
Which has enabled our species to survive
And to flourish in every corner of the earth.
For alone we are vulnerable, even helpless,
But compassion makes possible our cooperation
And successful our relationships, even beautiful,
Freeing the full expression of our personalities
And our finest and noblest of qualities.

We are distinct from the rest of life
By our greater capacity for both love and hate, good and evil.
But only when we are distinguished by compassion
Can we find our enlightenment,
Establish just economies
And move toward the ideal
Of a peaceful global village.

VOICE 1:
It is compassion that compels us
To alleviate the suffering
Of all our fellow creatures,
Of the lands, the seas, and the skies,
And to honor the sanctity of all humankind
With equity, justice, and respect.
Compassion calls us
To refrain from causing harm,
To cultivate empathy and understanding,
To speak out against violence,

Against greed and bigotry,
Poverty and exploitation,
And every violation of human rights
Whether in near or distant lands,
To end and heal the misery
Inflicted in the name of religion
And to reject those scriptures
Or interpretations of scripture
That incite hatred, violence, and disdain
And spur the self-righteous on
In their conceit.

The God of love requires us
To set the principle of compassion
At the heart of our faith
And at the heart of every ethical
And spiritual tradition.
In our teaching and our practice
And at the fore and front line
Of every battle
We seek out evidence
Of the God of compassion
In the Bible and other literature,
In Christian experience
And in other faiths,
So that we might pool
The wisdom of our species
And grow in spiritual maturity.
We affirm the power and centrality
Of love and compassion
In our Christian faith
And the possibilities for our transformation
Individually and corporately
Into a loving and considerate people
Holding right actions more sacred
Than "right" beliefs.

Voice 2:
Empower us, O God,
To spread abroad
Accurate and respectful information
To educate the world's youth
About the "other,"
Other peoples and cultures,
Religions and philosophies,
So they might learn
To appreciate diversity
Without seeing enemies
Where there are friends,
So they might learn to identify
With the pain of all humanity,
Both ally and adversary,
The strange and the familiar.
For an absence of compassion
Is most often the outcome
Of a lack of knowledge
And a poor grasp of the facts
Of wrong beliefs that flow
From ignorance and superstition.
So we pray to our God of highest intelligence,
The mind behind all that we are and see,
To divulge the secrets of reality
As we labor in thought and laboratory
So that ignorance and fear
Can no longer be given as excuses
For prejudice and chauvinism.

Only compassion brings down
The walls that divide us,
Helping us to see what we have in common
And to live peaceably with our neighbors,
And when there is real difference
To tolerate with patience the intolerant

And those who lack compassion,
Exerting force against them only
When they cause or threaten to cause
Harm to one another, others, or ourselves
Or break the rule of law where it is just.
We act in kindness toward such people, and wait
Until there is a chance to break through
To reach beyond toleration
To collaboration and friendship.

Still-Speaking Parable:
The Assassin

VOICE 3:
Someone had been watching the Great Leader, and not for the spectacle of his entourage passing by. There were many who might track his movements. Some looked for the chance of self-promotion through association, others for a moment of weakness in his defenses so that they might take their revenge. These particular watching eyes, however, were different, intent in their hostility beyond anything the Great Leader had imagined possible. The ownership of them remained an enigma, partly because they belonged to an otherwise veiled figure but mostly because the Great Leader had wronged so many in his time, burning down villages, ravaging and pillaging, all for the sake of conquest and dominion.

As the Great Leader grew old, the sightings became more frequent and the eyes began to bore deeper and deeper into his consciousness until he became paranoid, seeing them even in sleep. The Great Leader knew it was only a matter of time before his past would catch up with him. Despite the power he conveyed in pomp and ceremony, he knew the determination of those eyes would always be greater than the will of his mercenaries to protect him. One day they would find him vulnerable and their gaze would consume him.

Sure enough, on a hot and humid evening as the guards were drifting in and out of sleep, and the Great Leader studied his tired features, alone in his private chamber, he suddenly caught a glimpse of a reflection not his own. A violent spasm in his chest seemed to choke him before he could even think, as if his very organs had been waiting for this moment, but he remained still, frozen. There in a corner of the glass were the eyes, unblinking and opaque, but close enough now that the Great Leader could at last unravel the mystery. He had seen these eyes, many years before. They had belonged to a small boy, a boy who stood among the embers of his village as it burned, fixing the Great Leader with a stare as he and his men drove away with their plunder. It was unusual for the Great Leader to leave behind survivors, even children, so the tiny defiant figure had lodged itself somewhere in his memory.

As the Great Leader's thoughts turned to his imminent death, the haunting eyes of this now mature and powerfully built man also looked into the mirror and noticed a reflection not their own, but that of an old, frail, and frightened man, not a man drunk on the spoils of war, but the brittle, empty shell of someone that once was but had not been for a very long time. It was, to his surprise, not so different from his own reflection and loomed like a ghastly vision of the future, for his own hatred had exceeded even that of the Great Leader's during his rampages through the land, torching and murdering villagers. It was as if the two forms of man, young and old, had merged; as if their present experience and feelings were one.

The young man remembered who he had been all those years ago on the eve of that terrible night of screaming and fire when he had first seen the Great Leader in the flesh. He had been a quiet and kindly boy who spent the days helping his parents cultivate the land. He wondered what kind of child the Great Leader, also a farmer's son, had been at that age. The gaze of both men met via the gold-framed portal of glass and held fast for a time as they both saw themselves in the other. A spark of compassion for two small boys, though both long dead, flickered in the deep cold of the young man's heart. It was fragile but insistent, and enough to set his feet in motion as they turned and fled the mansion as secretively as they had entered.

Invitation

While the music is playing, you are invited to think and pray about how you will address any areas or circumstances in which you may be slow to compassion. You are welcome to light a candle as a symbol of your renewed resolve to act compassionately.

VOICE 1:
Forgive us, God of mercies,
When we are slow to compassion
And distant from those who need us.

**As we would have others do unto us,
Let us do unto them the same.**

VOICE 2:
When we are impatient,

Give us grace;

VOICE 1:
When we are hard of heart,

Give us tenderness;

VOICE 2:
When we are critical,

Give us kindness.

VOICE 1:
We say together the prayer of Jesus:

**Our father in heaven,
Holy is your name.
Your kingdom come.
Your will be done
On earth as it is in heaven.
Give us this day
Our daily bread,
And forgive us our debts
As we forgive our debtors.
Lead us not into temptation**

But deliver us from evil,
For yours is the kingdom,
The power, and the glory,
Now and forever.
Amen.

Communion

VOICE 1:
 Seeing a people weary
Of political and social unrest,
Of religious conformity and coercion,
Of violence and uncertainty,
A people ground in the mill of poverty
And hollowed out by drudgery,
A people without moral compass
Aimlessly wandering,
Blind after blind,
A thirsty shepherdless flock
Confused and dispirited,
Ravaged by demon and disease,
A society where half its population
Was marked out from birth
And diminished by intimidation and suppression
According to their gender and the ignorance of men,
It came to pass that one man, a mere carpenter,
Was struck to the heart
By the tragedy of the human condition
And moved by a compassion so great
That he gave up everything to find for us
A means of deliverance.
Undergoing a passion all his own,
He took upon his very flesh
And upon his inward soul
Every evil that befalls humankind
And every pain that afflicts,
From physical injury to humiliation,
From mental anguish to despair.

He faced the nadir of the living and the dead,
Resisting evil without the sword,
To vindicate our will to overcome,
Proving it to be no mere vanity
But a trust in the goodness of God,
For beyond every suffering there is peace,
Beyond every sin, forgiveness,
Beyond even death, life.

In Christ God extends to us
The hand of friendship,
The assurance that our trust will deliver
So we might draw nearer still
And know what it means to come home,
To belong in communion,
And to celebrate that closeness,
Taking God to our flesh as the bread is eaten
And to our hearts as the wine is drunk.

VOICE 2:
Author of life, surround this nourishment of body and soul,
Making these [*gesture toward the elements*]
the emblem of all you have accomplished
In a broken body and blood that was shed.

Raising and breaking the bread

This is the bread of your renewing;
It is broken that you may know the fullness of life.

Raising the cup of wine

This is the blood-wine of your salvation;
It is poured out so that you may know healing and peace.

The bread is passed around the group with the words:

The body of Christ, for your fullness of life.

The wine is passed around the group with the words:

The blood of Christ, for your healing and peace.

A time of silence is kept.

VOICE 1:
O God, be the eternal comfort of my people
And the well-being of my own soul.
Finding you over the horizon of every sorrow
Is salvation in itself,
A relief more wonderful
Than all the pleasures of the world,
For you do not abandon us
To an indifferent or hostile universe
But uphold us, as our very breath,
As the energy that animates,
As the elements from which we were formed.
You are the one who reaches out,
Snatching us from the jaws of malice
And dragging us from the mud
Even when our bodies are limp
And our minds in a fog of grief and exhaustion.
When we are riddled with decay or depravity,
When we are mute with shame,
Or consumed by hatreds and regrets,
You find the core of gold amid the dross,
The seed that may yet grow tall and swollen with fruit.
For you renew our opportunities
With each rising of the sun
And know the heart of the penitent
From that of the pretender,
Welcoming home always
To the fold of the saints
Those that seek you for healing
Or call to you for forgiveness.

And so it was that Jesus asked us to remember him
And all he stood for and died to bring about
In the simple act of sharing bread and wine,
Reminding us that principles must be practiced in community

Or they remain illusory, apparitions of the mind.
For the sharing of food and drink
Ensures our coming together
So that mutuality can draw out the best from each of us,
Exceeding all that we can be and do alone,
That we might glorify God to the fullest
With every atom of our being,
For it is only in companionship
That we find ourselves complete.

Meditation on Scripture

VOICE 4:

The Parable of the Good Samaritan, Luke 10:25–37

Just then a lawyer stood up to test Jesus. "Teacher," he said, "what must I do to inherit eternal life?" He said to him, "What is written in the law? What do you read there?" He answered, "You shall love the Lord your God with all your heart, and with all your soul, and with all your strength, and with all your mind; and your neighbor as yourself." And he said to him, "You have given the right answer; do this, and you will live."

But wanting to justify himself, he asked Jesus, "And who is my neighbor?" Jesus replied, "A man was going down from Jerusalem to Jericho, and fell into the hands of robbers, who stripped him, beat him, and went away, leaving him half dead. Now by chance a priest was going down that road; and when he saw him, he passed by on the other side. So likewise a Levite, when he came to the place and saw him, passed by on the other side. But a Samaritan while travelling came near him; and when he saw him, he was moved with pity. He went to him and bandaged his wounds, having poured oil and wine on them. Then he put him on his own animal, brought him to an inn, and took care of him. The next day he took out two denarii, gave them to the innkeeper, and said, 'Take care of him; and when I come back, I will repay you whatever more you spend.' Which of these three, do you think, was a neighbor to the man who fell into the hands of the robbers?" He said, "The one who showed him mercy." Jesus said to him, "Go and do likewise."

Sung Refrain

Final Prayer and Blessing

VOICE 2:
God of creation,
Make us a people of sympathy,

A people of loving-kindness.

VOICE 2:
God of incarnation,
Make us a people of empathy,

A people of understanding.

VOICE 2:
Hear the call to a life of compassion,
A life neither foolish nor dull,

For goodness is no solemn vow
But a fullness of life
And love.

VOICE 1:
Love divine, love excelling,
Love compelling us to meet,
Move within us to embrace
The humble and proud,
The tearful and smiling,
To share the load, to stand beside,

**To bring our heavenly home
Toward its earthly rest.**

Invitation

Take time over refreshments after the service to share ideas for developing compassionate living in your own community, at work, at church, and at leisure.

Bible texts for use in the Meditations on Scripture include Luke 4:18–19 with Isaiah 61 (Jesus' Gospel), Matthew 22:34–40 (The greatest commandment), Mark 12:28–34 (The first commandment), Mark 2:13–17 (Jesus calls Levi), Luke 15:1–10 (The parables of the lost sheep and lost coin), Matthew 9:35–38 (The harvest is great, the laborers few), John 8:1–11 (The woman caught in adultery), Luke 7:36–50 (A woman forgiven), and Matthew 12:9–14 (The man with the withered hand).

FOUR

Salvation

The *Liturgy of Salvation* is suitable for use during the period of Easter and is called at that time *The Easter Liturgy of Resurrection*. It includes an optional baptismal service with sections for both adult and infant baptismal candidates which can be used according to the preferred tradition of your community. Included in the latter is an appreciation of motherhood, fatherhood, and thanksgiving for the family. The adult baptismal liturgy celebrates not just the coming of age of the teenager brought up in a Christian home, who has decided to continue as a disciple of Christ, but the faith commitment of any adult who wishes to be symbolically and sacramentally grafted into the community of disciples.

The event is a symbol and a public declaration of that candidate's experience of salvation and of the death and resurrection of Christ. It is a sacramental event in that it is a deeply affirming and transformative experience of unity and belonging and, in some cases, healing and liberation—all things that constitute a further experience of salvation. In infant baptism, the child is also welcomed into the body of the church universal as a new disciple of Christ according to the wishes of his or her parents. Though the infant may be unaware of the meaning of the proceedings, the experience is nonetheless symbolic of Christ's death and resurrection, of the beginning of discipleship and of God's love and welcome for all humanity.

The baptismal event is also sacramental in the experience of the family and community witnessing it. Importantly, this liturgy also gives provision for the confirmation of faith and the renewal of baptismal vows for all others present. This liturgy, in particular, may be characterized by a sense of drama, theater, and action while maintaining the gentle rhythms and silences appropriate for reflective thought. A reflective liturgy provides an opportunity for a more intimate and thoughtful baptismal ceremony as an alternative to one carried out in the more frenetic and impersonal atmosphere of ordinary services. It is important to note that it is perfectly reasonable for persons baptized as infants to be baptized again when they come of age and recommit themselves to God and the church as teenagers or adults. This is especially the case if the principles of the original baptism were not followed through by the parents in some way that is significant for the individual or if the person has since their initial baptism experienced a time of alienation from God or the church and now wishes to publicly express a renewed commitment.

While cultivating compassion brings healing, both lead to the ultimate goal of faith, which is salvation. A state of being healed is salvation, but it comes in many forms, including liberation from oppression, injustice, and poverty, the transforming power of knowledge through education that leads to truth or enlightenment, and a contentment that comes with knowing one is home and safe in the loving presence and permanence of God. Salvation is the state of being that faces death without fear and dread because of a sense of one's eternal, unbreakable communion with God. It overcomes the fear of what is unknown and provides a deeper sense of security than anything the physical world could give us. Such a feeling is echoed in the words of Paul the apostle in Romans 8:35–39:

> Who will separate us from the love of Christ? Will hardship, or distress, or persecution, or famine, or nakedness, or peril, or sword? As it is written, "For your sake we are being killed all day long; we are accounted as sheep to be slaughtered." No, in all these things we are more than conquerors through him who loved us. For I am convinced that neither death, nor life, nor angels, nor rulers, nor things present, nor things to come, nor powers, nor height, nor depth, nor anything else in all creation, will be able to separate us from the love of God in Christ Jesus our Lord.

Salvation is one of the greatest insights of the religious traditions because it acknowledges the reality of profound changes within a person that can permanently alter their life, their attitudes, lifestyle, morality, and capacity for love and compassion. This is something secular societies can be skeptical and suspicious about, and it is hard to blame them when there have been fraudulent claims in this vein, especially among a prison population hoping to be granted leniency in their sentencing. However, there are also those of us who have experienced a conversion in adulthood and are familiar with our own and others' dramatic and undoubtedly real transformations.

An experience of divine revelation has the power to turn even the most hardened of human hearts, and with astonishing speed, as happened to Paul of Tarsus on the road to Damascus. It is as a light that suddenly shines in the mind and heart of a person and banishes the darkness that was there. Conversions are often described as a commissioning, in which one is chosen for a particular purpose, and as redemptive, in which one is plucked out of depravity or despair by the hand of a God, a hand that will not let go. These experiences are often accompanied by feelings of euphoria and inner peace.

The theology of salvation (known as soteriology) has to be central to the new, progressive theology. It is important to note that the salvation experience, in the variety of forms I have mentioned above (including dramatic and instantaneous conversion experiences), traverses the boundaries of culture and religion, and we must move away from the assumption that as Christians, we are the only people to have experienced them. This does not mean there is nothing unique about Christian revelation in the context of that experience. In fact, Christianity is distinct in the degree of its fascination with one particular aspect of salvation: the release from one's own tendency toward certain evils. This is what, for the Christian, precipitates a new ability to forgive oneself and others, to feel unprecedented warmth or love for others, and escape the vicious cycles of vengeance and rivalry that are so universally human. One is forever conscious of a God outside oneself, reminding us of that life-changing moment of liberation, and strengthening us to continue in this new way, free from the bad habits of the past.

This focus of Christianity is of course centered on the cross and atonement, the way that Jesus' death has been thought to deal with sin. Much of church history has been steeped in the idea that Jesus was the perfect sacrifice, a ransom demanded by the devil which God had to pay to redeem or buy us back, or that the sacrifice of Jesus was necessary to restore God's honor because God had been dishonored by the sins of humanity, or that Jesus was the one chosen as a substitute, to bear the punishment from God that we deserved for our sin. The latter two of course imply that God had no choice but to mete out justice by means of violence and death, because under some universal law, sin could only be absolved (or honor restored) by the death of an innocent. These views of a God under law, a God with a vain obsession with his own honor, and a God beholden to the devil, are all very human, even comically so, but are very low and unsatisfactory estimations of the character and power of God. However, there has long been a better alternative to such beliefs: the view that because of Jesus' resurrection or immortality in the vibrancy of the faith and community that he founded, his death on the cross marks a definitive victory over suffering and death and over the heights of human evil and brutality in the torturing and killing of one of their own.

It is in fact Jesus' life that marks the greatest victory over sin, because it is he who in the end has given more people the message of God's willingness to forgive the repentant, and who has provided the teachings and example for us to lead a morally good life, more so than almost anyone else who has ever lived. Though it is important to move away from an obsession with sin in the church at the expense of the other aspects of salvation, the overcoming of our sinful nature and liberation from guilt remain important aspects of our spirituality and a special concern for the Christian.

The *Liturgy of Salvation* takes inspiration from the vision of the faithful of our final end, one that has taken many forms, the main one in Christianity being our entrance into an idyllic place known as heaven, a metaphor, or rather one of a number of biblical metaphors, for the ideal society, world, or cosmos. It also recognizes the inward, sometimes instant, sometimes gradual experiences of oneness with God and creation that have the power to change lives, as well as the equally transformative and saving experiences of physical liberation and healing, while also exploring our longer struggle or journey toward a complete salvation in which our longings to be saved in all these different ways are at last fulfilled.

It is important here to note the mutual dependence of different salvation experiences. One might be receptive to inward change, but if this can have no outward consequences because one is overwhelmed by physical or mental suffering, one's experience of salvation will be greatly diminished or even made impossible. The experience of salvation would be equally worthless if liberation from oppression or ignorance were achieved without an inner moral and spiritual transformation, for history would simply repeat itself with evil perpetuated as victims become villains in search of vengance. For this reason it is important that the outlook of the Christian and the church on humanity should always be holistic, neither biased toward evangelism (the sharing of our Gospel message and experiences of inner change) nor toward social and humanitarian work. These aspects of humanity simply cannot be separated and must be addressed together.

The *Liturgy of Salvation* grounds us in our individual and common purpose as people of faith. It reminds us of our need for this broader purpose, beyond mere work or leisure, or reproducing or attempting to immortalize ourselves. This goal of salvation is a great insight of religion that has inspired enormous creativity, including creativity for its own sake because this ability is what defines us as bearers of God's image since God is the spirit of creativity sustaining all of life. Religion concentrates on meaning, the expression and journey of the inner self, and maintains a profoundly hopeful outlook on life. This liturgy considers more fully our individual spiritual growth and direction while balancing this with our need for collective salvation.

It is all about continual renewal and regeneration as much as about any particular salvation event, and it is about rejoicing and celebrating with those who have shared in these experiences. It is a celebration of the power of the Christian message of resurrection that is still very much alive around the world today, as well as of the new life and light that returns each year with the spring. Jesus was, after all, the most prominent if not the only spiritual leader who according to tradition claimed to be the life and light of the world and who is still believed to be that life and light by more than a third of the world's population:

> Again Jesus spoke to them, saying, "I am the light of the world. Whoever follows me will never walk in darkness but will have the light of life." (John 8:12)

> Jesus said to him [Thomas], "I am the way, and the truth, and the life. No one comes to the Father except through me." (John 14:6)

The latter verse has often been used to claim exclusivity for the Christian faith as the only way to salvation. The underlying assumptions of course are that these were the actual words of Jesus, that they apply for all of time and space, and that Jesus himself was infallible. However, even if one were to agree with these assumptions, when one reads verses like this without a background of indoctrination and thus a bias already in place, one can see that the author's meaning was that Jesus, as an incarnation of God, had the power to decide who would be welcomed into the presence of that God.

The author does not mean that throughout all ages and lands it is only those who believe that Jesus is the son of God—in terms of being the full and only manifestation of God—who will go to heaven. The prevalent but mistaken understanding of verses like this has sadly obscured the true meaning and context of these sayings and encouraged Christians to believe that they rather than Jesus can decide who is in and who is out of God's favor, according to whether or not a person gives assent to particular statements of doctrine. The result is that they become the broadcasters of bad rather than good news, the bad news of who is unwelcome in God's presence, which turns out to be very bad news since that includes almost everyone except themselves and perhaps a few congregations identical to theirs. This is compounded by the even worse news that to remedy their situation the great masses of "unsaved" must believe a long list of highly implausible and suspect things.

The much happier reality, however, is that it is as it has always been, only the Holy Spirit of God whose judgment matters, the spirit of God, known to some in a risen Christ, who still lives and breathes that spirit in the hearts and the imaginations of many. This is truly great news, since the God of Jesus has been described through the ages and in many cultures as the God of love who is long-suffering, patient, generous, relenting, gracious, forgiving, and desirous of the salvation of all.

This God is not like a court judge who is remote and indifferent to our fate, requiring from us the fulfillment of certain legal or ritualistic obligations, or indeed mental gymnastics to produce belief, conformity of thought, or behavior, or some kind of contrived emotional response. God is instead like a mother, a comforter, and one who gives much and demands little. Even those in biblical times who often conceived of a hot-tempered and endlessly dissatisfied God at a deeper level knew this:

> He has told you, O mortal, what is good; and what does the Lord require of you but to do justice, and to love kindness, and to walk humbly with your God? (Mic. 6:8)

> For thus says the Lord: I will extend prosperity to her like a river, and the wealth of the nations like an overflowing stream; and you shall nurse and be carried on her arm, and dandled on her knees. As a mother comforts her child, so I will comfort you; you will be comforted in Jerusalem. (Isa. 66:12–13)

Christians have long held the resurrection to be the cornerstone of the faith, though they have long debated the nature of that event. Some are convinced of a physical, bodily resurrection, others of a more metaphorical understanding of the events described in the Gospels. Whatever one's view, and in spite of all the questions surrounding the origins of the sayings and stories of the New Testament, a person named Jesus, who died two thousand years ago and to whom those sayings are attributed, lives on in the minds and hearts of billions of Christians and in the example of many followers of the way that have gone before us.

This Jesus whether a spirit, fleshly or imagined being, remains as real a force in our world as any other force, and a manifestation of God that invites all of us, without exception, and on equal terms, to come to him for our spiritual resting place, and to quench our thirst in the rivers of eternal life:

Jesus said to her, "Everyone who drinks of this water will be thirsty again, but those who drink of the water that I will give them will never be thirsty. The water that I will give will become in them a spring of water gushing up to eternal life." (John 4:13–14)

Come to me, all you that are weary and carrying heavy burdens, and I will give you rest. Take my yoke upon you, and learn from me; for I am gentle and humble in heart, and you will find rest for your souls. For my yoke is easy, and my burden is light. (Matt. 11:28–30)

Jesus is so very captivating precisely because he is a personal manifestation of a transcendent, impersonal God who would otherwise remain an abstract concept, a fleeting indefinable thought in the mind. Not only was he a person as we commonly understand a person to be, human, creaturely, and able to interact with other persons, but he also used the intimate term Abba (Father) for God, which demonstrated a familial relationship, one that is about uninhibited speaking and listening—in other words, about prayer.

This concept of prayer is very different from that state in which one merely observes and contemplates divinity—a state valid in itself but limited. Jesus' life in conversation with God, especially during times such as his isolation in the desert and his agony in the garden, affirmed the credibility of our own prayer lives, our own compulsion to speak to God in our own languages in times of immense gratitude or suffering. He gives us courage to think of our prayers as more powerful and consequential than what we would otherwise consider to be the mere conversations we have within ourselves that may or may not help to resolve difficulties and enable us to cope better with life.

For prayer, though strange and inexplicable, whether silent or aloud, remains one of the most instinctive and intuitive aspects of human behavior, traversing all boundaries of culture or creed. Even some of the most fervent atheists have been known to pray, albeit in extreme circumstances. Like the call to ministry, the call to prayer is a peculiar and seemingly even a foolish one, since at a level beneath the simplest of definitions it has to be irrational. The supposed consequences of prayer, or God's "answers," appear to be unpredictable or even arbitrary if they are to be discerned by reason at all. However, at some level of our being, from one day to the next all human beings are irrational. Our consciousness is not so sophisticated that we can exist and act in every moment according to universal laws of logic and reason.

An extent of irrationality is, therefore, unavoidable until perhaps some future time when we might be able to enhance our brains artificially! It is for this reason that prayer, though often described as difficult because of its slippery nature when we reflect on it, actually comes more easily to us in terms of practice than we might expect, even to the most logically minded. When methods of prayer are practiced they become easier still, and their benefits for our well-being are almost universally acknowledged. It is the transformation of the self through prayer that constitutes its power. Human irrationality, though often a curse, can in some circumstances be a blessing and underpins a form of adult play that is necessary for imaginative and creative thinking: thinking that is free from the restraints of convention and dogma and perceives new connections and patterns.

The liturgies in this book help to introduce and develop some of the methods of prayer that are the bedrock of our spirituality. The listening aspect of prayer is best cultivated through such things as the awareness meditations described in the final chapter, in the meditations on scripture, the still-speaking parables, the poetry, and the frequent silences. The speaking aspect of prayer is drawn out and guided by the liturgy itself and in the sung refrains or songs of devotion. These are not, of course, meant to replace but to supplement personal extempore prayer. Longer silences have a special place in every liturgy, encouraging participants to take the initiative and engage in free rather than guided prayer. Lessons in the practice of prayer are at the heart of Christian spirituality and must therefore be the heart of this book.

THE LITURGY OF SALVATION

The central table could display spring flowers or potted seedlings or saplings which guests can take away at the end to grow indoors or plant in their gardens as an exercise in nurturing life.

Welcome

VOICE 1:
Christ is risen in triumph over death!

Arise all creation in joyful response!

Christ is risen in triumph over sin!

Arise now, disciples, and follow him!

Look to the horizon where a new day dawns!

**For flinging wide its gates within us
Is the glorious realm of God!**

Sung Refrain

VOICE 2:
Consider the question that is God,
And take courage to answer it,
For your names and mine are written
Upon that great eternal mind,
And we stand in nature's holy temple
Preparing in worship
For lives and worlds anew.

**We take it to our hearts,
The question that is God,
And respond with our feet.
Though the road is rough and long
And the tolls are high,
We will not be afraid to fall,**

For faltering brings wisdom
Which in time is sure to reap
The greater harvest.
So we make bold our experiment in life,
Rooted in our trust and hope,
That every moment is held secure
In the bounds of divine love.

Poem:
The Strangest of Faiths

VOICE 3:
What kind of faith is this?
A man sent from God,
wholly flesh,
One in three
. . . and what kind of path?
One I could choose,
but not without grace,
that chooses me.
They told me the story,
but I couldn't see.

What kind of life is this?
With One who knows all,
yet calls me to pray,
wants me to agree.
. . . and what kind of hope?
Where won battles rage,
heaven's realm is here,
but there's one yet to be.
They told me the story,
but I couldn't see.

What kind of power is this?
A ruler who serves.
A God who suffers,
to set me free.

. . . and what kind of questioner am I?
On bended knee
And equally
A mystery.
They told me the story,
but I couldn't see.

What knowledge can then save?
Except for the kind
that both is and is not
depending on Thee.
. . . and what of Revelation?
A season of love,
A thing called reality?
I opened my eyes,
to ephemeral skies,
And I couldn't see.
Can the Word believed then save?

No mere assent of mind,
but in love we find
our home in Thee.
. . . and what of God's story?
Of lives lived, yet living,
for an eternity.
The good yet beyond me
Resounds in the heavens
And only in its wake, I see.

(Written in 2007 and published in an earlier version in *Life and Work,*
the Church of Scotland magazine in 2009)

Still-Speaking Parable:
A Testimony

VOICE 4:

It was then that I knew you, looking out at a distant and craggy hilltop, the colors of nature strangely vivid, resplendent. Within, the raging waters of my soul, for a moment calmed, were reflective as glass. And so it was that you became apparent in them, in a place where there had been darkness and pain, and I gazed into your immeasurable depths from some new plane of consciousness.

Were we the only ones for whom the cosmos had shifted? I now orbited a new world, like a satellite, thrown from its trajectory by some mighty impact, an unbreakable gravity between us. Of course your presence, not wholly unfamiliar, had always been with me, watching patiently at my back. But it was in the beginnings of healing, in release from fear, fear that wrought only the tragedy of wasted life, that the path to enlightenment stretched out before me. I began to tread the pilgrim way, held safe in my salvation, the eternal balm of God.

For the first time, I knew the greatness of your love, a love without condition, unflinching in the face of my inmost thoughts and desires. It was that grace astounding, spoken of by those who walked this way before. One can only describe this love in terms of God, for there is no other good enough to give it. The truth of your love, confirmed in that moment, freed my soul from the doubtful hoping of an aching heart that searches long and wearily before it finds. Loosed into worship, reborn for joy, that heart now skipped, as if the vibrant atomic world had begun to pulsate with unprecedented vigor. As to the senses of an infant, even the minutiae of reality dazzled. They enchanted an imagination no longer veiled in the mists of adulthood's accumulated delusions.

I reveled in the vision of you, until it faded imperceptibly, but the memory of it stayed with me, a portrait in the mind. So did my new belonging and purpose, as if my every molecule had been realigned by some vast magnetic field, pointing doggedly toward a new destiny. I no longer feared the future, regretted my failings, or counted my deficiencies; they were no longer obstacles but windows into one on whom I now depended, reminding me to place my hope in something greater than I. They would become the surprising conduits for a love unattenuated by the ego. The passage of time would prove your love unfailing, again and again, even when my trust in it proved, in contrast, to be contingent on the passing of the seasons, brittle and wavering.

Who would be my guide, I wondered, someone to speak to me in my own language within these limited dimensions of which we mortals are aware? Who would be the light en route to that paradise of my momentary glimpsing? Then, out of the pages of scripture came one who claimed to be a light for all the world and spoke powerfully of a new order that would rise out of chaos, founded on principles of equality, justice, and peace. Here was someone who emboldened me to strive for a greater good, the good that I longed for but had been afraid to do and to be, in case it proved foolish, meaningless. Here was someone who told of an all-consuming love, such as had apprehended me, a love that will make its home in our midst requiring neither temple nor earthly mediator for its channeling.

I recognized in Jesus the God I had encountered—in his character, full of compassion and kindness, in the moral acuity of the parables, and in his descriptions of a realm of God emerging already among us. It would have seemed idealistic, even naive but for the encounter that permanently altered the course of my life, one which I shared with the disciples of Jesus in rare intimacy across the ages. I took the unplanned, even compulsive decision to join that motley multitude, a decision I never regretted. Jesus' teachings became for me a prism by which truth is refracted into its many splendid colors.

The impact of his life and death made him a nexus between the material and spiritual, the great fission in our time and space by which God broke through and was revealed to humankind more fully than ever before. And so it was that Christianity, with its most paradoxical and peculiar collection of people and stories, became my spiritual resting place and the vehicle for living out my salvation.

Invitation

While the music is playing, ponder the insights and experiences that have led (or may be leading) you to trust in God, while giving due attention to any doubts and uncertainties you may have. You are welcome to light a candle as a symbol of your renewed trust.

Communion

VOICE 1:
The character of God is made known to us,
Not in one way but in many,
In encounters with divinity
And our moments of insight,
In a sense of divine presence and calling,
In inspired writings, scriptures, and sayings
And the literature of the wise.
It is revealed in nature,
Observed through eye and measure,
In reason and the patterns of numbers,
But perhaps the greatest revelation of all
For those belonging to the Christian way
Is the life, death, and resurrection of Christ,
A window on the face of God.

VOICE 2:
Though we condemn the innocent and trample the weak,
Forsaking them as Christ was forsaken even by his friends,
God protects the noble and their cause
With a mighty affirmation,
Anointing subversives when they lead the struggle
For liberation and justice.
Like Christ they are beloved of God and held in high esteem,
And God seals their victory in the transformation of the world,
Just as a glorious victory was revealed at the cross
Over all existing powers and systems of domination
In a cosmic drama in which Christ became the victor
Over wickedness and death.

VOICE 1:
In life, Jesus revealed the most excellent way,
A dying to the old self that gives breath to the new.
His cross revealed the towering heights
To which humanity can rise,
Our great capacity for good,
For when united with him

In his mission and love for all creation
We take on the challenges of our time
And confront the powers that keep us apart,
Searching for the path to becoming one
As we let go of self in the mystery of union with God.

Voice 2:
The cross reveals unimaginable depths
Of God's great love for humanity,
For even as we crushed the innocent and the poor,
Averting our eyes from God in rejection of all her goodness,
And while the worst of our venom spilled over,
She reached out to us in Christ,
Who threw himself onto the tree of death
And upon God's mercy.
For in complete abandonment he died
In agony because of us and for us,
Both friend and foe.

Voice 1:
So we ask that this physical act of communion
Be a means to perceive the mysteries of our God
And a reminder of the central story of our faith,
The story of Jesus in his life and death.

The leader raises the bread and wine and all say:

We invoke the Holy Spirit!
Come upon this bread and this wine in grace and power!

Voice 1:
On the night that Jesus was betrayed, he took bread and gave thanks to
God. Sharing the bread with his disciples, he said, "Take and eat, this
is my body given for you: Do this in remembrance of me."
After supper, he took the cup and again gave thanks to God. He said to
his disciples, "Drink this, all of you: this is my blood, the blood of the
new covenant, shed for you and for many, for the forgiveness of sins.
Do this in remembrance of me."

The bread is broken and distributed with the words:

The body of Christ, broken in love.

The wine is shared with the words:

The blood of Christ, shed in forgiveness.

A time of silence is kept.

VOICE 2:
For the Jews in the time of Jesus,
Divine forgiveness and purification
Could only take place at the temple,
And only by this forgiveness and cleansing
Could a Jew enter the presence of God.
Thus on the Day of Atonement
The sins and impurities of all people and creation
Were borne away by priest, sacrifice, and scapegoat,
And ultimately by the Lord their God.
Those who were disciples of Jesus,
Knew him in terms of all of these,
Jesus the sacrificial lamb, the scapegoat, and high priest
Surrendering his life for the cause of God,
And in defiance of human sin
Banished, cursed, and despised in their stead,
A mediator, through his astonshing act of selfless giving,
Reconciling their people with a God from whom they felt alienated,
On account of their evil deeds.
And as he died willingly, and an innocent
Christ became for some their ultimate sacrifice,
Freeing them forever from their heavy burden of guilt
And tearing the temple curtain in two.
Their access to God would no longer be restricted
By cleric, temple, or tradition
Or any other power,
For Christ brought an end to the sacrificial system
And declared humanity

No longer divided or distant from God
But swept to her heart in an amazing grace
More radical and total than they had ever known.

VOICE 1:
For every good cause a sacrifice is made,
The struggle that precedes every triumph,
The knowing of pain behind every kindness,
And in Christ was a sacrifice
Revealing God's affinity
With all our struggles and pain.
It would bring not just the Jews
But all of humanity nearer to God,
Freeing us from the ruin of guilt,
To know what is required of us:
An embrace of divine imperatives,
The laws of compassion and love.

And the sacrifice of Christ
Urges us to take courage ourselves,
To make our own sacrifices
For the greater good of all,
So that no one might be lost in confusion
But all might find God's way and purpose,
Integrating the body, mind, and soul
And leading to the fulfillment
Of our greatest potential.
For in Christ God offers immeasurable blessing
Extended with unparalleled generosity
Throughout the universe,
The known and the unknown,
And to every human heart.

Prayers of Occasion

VOICE 1:
From calamity, adversity, and suffering ***save us!***
From hatred, persecution, and hopelessness ***save us!***

Bring us out to pasture
In a spacious place,
For we are heavy laden
With troubles great and small.
But the yoke of God is easy,
And the burden of God is light.

VOICE 2:
From selfishness, greed, and prejudice *save us!*
From captivity, oppression, and subordination *save us!*

For you delight to set us free,
To rejoice in our God always,
To work and play, and sleep soundly,
To laugh and cry without fear,
For you will our emancipation,
Our struggles for equality,
Our protection under law,
And the education of all
That will end the curse of ignorance
And all its unhappy offspring.

VOICE 2:
Generous God,
We pray that we might offer this salvation hope
To all in our midst and beyond,
For the gift was never ours to keep for ourselves alone.
We renounce any narrow views of salvation that we might have had
And which came to dominate
The life and teachings of the church,
Beliefs which kept selfishly this gift,
Restricting the terms of salvation
According to the desires of the few,
So many found themselves excluded,
Casting into shadow our message of good news.
We relinquish those beliefs that split our minds in two,
One after the God of wisdom, gentleness, and compassion,

The other after a petulant and bloodthirsty God,
A God of anger and bitterness
Who cannot forgive at will
And is vengeful and jealous,
One who is bound by a law that demands
Innocent blood in exchange for forgiveness,
One who would punish his son to restore his own honor,
Or a God beholden to devils and evil powers,
Bargaining with the life of Christ to free us from their grasp.
We reject these beliefs that soured our view of God's character
And changed much of our kindness to contempt.

VOICE 1:
So help us instead to rediscover
The true meaning of the cross,
The revelation of what God is really like,
All-giving and all-welcoming,
Without allowing its brutality
To eclipse the life and teachings of Christ
And the joy and power of the resurrection,
In which death is superseded
By the restored lives of many.
Help us to appreciate again
The cosmic dimensions of redemption,
The salvation of all of creation
Often overlooked and ignored
In our blinkered focus on humanity.
Help us also to realize the elements of salvation
Beyond those that deal only with sin and guilt
So that we might know God in all freedom and truth,
In health, success, and homecoming
As well as in forgiveness and reconciliation.
Attune us, God of virtues,
To the wisdom of our consciences
And to our human sense of justice.
Keep them always loyal to divine compassion,

For though corruptible, they bear your image.
Uphold those scriptures that reflect your will,
Helping us to abandon those which do not.
For nothing of ours is perfect as you are perfect,
And all things must be weighed in the balance
So your middle way can be found.

VOICE 2:
We embrace salvation as transformation
Of body and soul, community and creation,
Sharing our experiences abroad
And adjusting our views as we learn.
We fine-tune our moral conscience,
Cultivating virtues through constant practice:
Prudence, the ability to judge how to act;
Justice, to moderate between self and others;
Temperance, to master our passions;
And fortitude, to meet every challenge
With endurance, courage, and strength.

We share our salvation with all those we meet
For even as we treasure the peace of God inwardly,
In the privacy of our own hearts and homes,
We acknowledge an immanent and transcendent God
Both within and beyond all of creation
Who calls us to take the message and means of salvation
To the lost, the enslaved, the suffering, and the oppressed,
So we might move with hope toward a better future
For the world of our awareness and the worlds beyond.

SERVICE OF BAPTISM— ADULT

VOICE 1:
Descend with us into the waters of baptism,
And rise with us into new life!

We join together in this sacrament:

A physical act that transforms the spirit,
Making right the attitudes of our hearts
And renewing us in vigor and hope.

Turning to the baptismal candidate:

This is the hour that you join with Christ in death and are reborn!

The candidate replies:

I am willing to enter the waters of death, leaving behind my old self and rising with Christ into new life!

The leader continues:

We are called to live in harmony with God and one another.
So I invite you to make baptismal vows in the sight of God and all here present, for these will be the foundation of your life to come.

The candidate makes the following vows:

1. I shall live to honor God who brings me my salvation.

2. I shall be faithful to God who is the source of all that is good.

3. I shall speak of God with respect and tell of God's glory.

4. I shall take time to rest and contemplate the wonders of God.

5. I shall honor all my family and treat them with loving-kindness.

6. I shall be merciful and compassionate toward other people, other animals and the earth, bringing them justice, healing, and peace, and refraining from doing them harm.

7. I shall be faithful to my wife/husband/partner/boyfriend/girl-friend, my family and my friends, knowing the richness that brings.

8. I shall respect the possessions of others, being honest in all my dealings.

9. I shall speak kindly of others and truthfully of myself.

10. I shall be content and generous with what I have, respecting and rejoicing in the success of others, while working hard to better myself.

We shall act justly, love mercy, and walk humbly with our God

> A parent may wish to read a poem or prayer for a teenager or youth at this point since their baptism also marks a coming of age. Below is a poem I have written as an example. A friend or relative of an older adult may also wish to make the personal contribution of a poem or prayer at this point.

For a Daughter or Son

There are many who would tell you to be silent,
Who would tell you that the battle can't be won;
That you do not have the strength to be a victor;
That alone, you have no choice but to run.

The cowards, they will brand you a maverick;
They would rather be conventional than just.
But you've something much more steely than the average,
So I'm giving you the treasure of my trust.

Though tall men stand before you, can you see?
For there'll be a way to navigate the throng.
Keep abreast of each unraveling mystery,
Bear the dark nights of your soul though they be long.

Take the spear and take the sword toward the fighting!
Take humility and a heavy heart there too.
Brave the world for many wrongs there call for righting,
And the victims wait for love, wait there for you.

Overcome? Then fall on me, your refuge place,
Here, none shall ever make my child afraid.
No specter at your heel, no haunted face.
Your mind's sweet respite from the devil's endless raid.

VOICE 2:
God of every precious soul,
Work in [*first name*]
To fix in *her/him*

This spoken commitment to your way.
Guide *his/her* every step,
Making every good thing
Spring from the covenant made this day.
Keep *her/him* true to *his/her* vows
In times of trial and temptation to wander,
In times of both joy and sadness,
So that *he/she* may stand before you
Till the end of *her/his* days
Honored among you and among us
As a valiant and faithful disciple
Bearing a torch and blazing a trail
For the goodness of God.
Amen.

The candidate is baptized with the words:

VOICE 1: [*Full name of the baptismal candidate*]
I baptize you in the name of our creator and redeemer,
The first and last and forever,
And in the name of the incarnation, Jesus Christ,
With the power of the Holy Spirit.
Amen.

A leader sprinkles the assembled company with water with the words:

Receive, all of you, the waters of life!

Or alternatively:

*You are invited to come forward for an anointing with water
(a cross of water on the forehead or palm).*

The following words can be used for the anointing: "Receive with
gladness the waters of life."

We will trust in God, the Author of Life,
With all the strength of our being
And commit to the way of life
Taught and shown to us in Christ.
Going with him into death
We set our faces against evil,
And reborn with him to a new life
We turn toward good and the way of love,
Running with the living water
That satisfies both body and soul.
And so we renew our baptismal vows
Filled afresh with the Spirit of God,
Seeking to realize our belonging,
Our becoming as one, the community of heaven.

Sung Refrain

SERVICE OF BAPTISM— INFANT

Voice 1:
Descend with us into the waters of baptism
And rise with us into new life!

We join together in this sacrament;
A physical act that transforms the spirit,
Making right the attitudes of our hearts
And renewing us in vigor and hope.

The infant baptismal candidate is taken into the arms of the leader who says the following prayer:

VOICE 1:
God of new life and of old,
Of our going out and coming in,
We present to you this child
[*full name*]
And ask that *she/he* be always yours,

For entering the waters of death
She/he will rise again into new life
And into unity with all the children of God
To live out *her/his* days in your presence,
Transformed by your Spirit of love.

We welcome you [*first name*]
To our family and church.
We will teach you and guide you
And share with you the earth
And all its treasures,
Striving to preserve them for you
And for all the generations yet to come
So you may see the marvels we have seen
And glorify God who gives them life.

VOICE 2:
We thank God for mothers and fathers,
For parental love, protection, and patient care.
Let us pray continually for their strength of will
To build homes of fairness and stability,
With consistency of discipline,
Where our children may thrive in peace
And certainty of love,
Where they may know tenderness and a listening ear
And enjoy freedom with wise counsel.
May [*first name*] be raised and grow willingly into a fine disciple
And a confident *brother/sister* of the way,
Respecting *herself/himself* and respecting all
And responding diligently and faithfully
To the call of God upon *his/her* life.

Remind us, God of wisdom,
To support (*first name*) in his/her journey,
In the peaks, troughs, and perplexities of life,
Welcoming *her/him* as our own
And protecting him /her from all harm,
For Jesus welcomed the little children

And said with unusual ferocity
That it would be better for a person to be drowned
Should they harm a child or lead him or her astray.
So we pray that God will make of us good examples
And trustworthy guides,
That our children may follow us
As we direct their feet,
That they might plant them aright
In the footsteps of Christ.

The infant is baptized with the words:

VOICE 1: [*Full name of the baptismal candidate*],
I baptize you in the name of our creator and redeemer,
The first and last and forever,
And in the name of the incarnation, Jesus Christ,
With the power of the Holy Spirit.
Amen.

A leader sprinkles the assembled company with water with the words:

Receive, all of you, the waters of life!

Or alternatively:

You are invited to come forward for an anointing with water (a cross of water on the forehead or palm).

> The following words can be used for the anointing: "Receive with gladness the waters of life."

We will trust in God, the Author of Life
With all the strength of our being
And commit to the way of life
Taught and shown to us in Christ.
Going with him into death,
We set our faces against evil,
And reborn with him to a new life

We turn toward good and the way of love,
Running with the living water
That satisfies both body and soul.
And so we renew our baptismal vows
Filled afresh with the Spirit of God,
Seeking to realize our belonging,
Our becoming as one, the community of heaven.

Meditation on Scripture

VOICE 3:

Psalm 116

I love the Lord, because he has heard
my voice and my supplications.
Because he inclined his ear to me,
therefore I will call on him as long as I live.
The snares of death encompassed me;
the pangs of Sheol laid hold on me;
I suffered distress and anguish.
Then I called on the name of the Lord:
"O Lord, I pray, save my life!"

Gracious is the Lord, and righteous;
our God is merciful.
The Lord protects the simple;
when I was brought low, he saved me.
Return, O my soul, to your rest,
for the Lord has dealt bountifully with you.

For you have delivered my soul from death,
my eyes from tears,
my feet from stumbling.
I walk before the Lord
in the land of the living.
I kept my faith, even when I said,

"I am greatly afflicted";
I said in my consternation,
"Everyone is a liar."

> Bible texts for use in the Meditations on Scripture include John
> 3:1–8 (Nicodemus visits Jesus), Psalm107, John 20:11–18 (Jesus
> appears to Mary Magdalene), John 20:19–23 (Jesus appears to the
> disciples), John 21:1–14 (Jesus appears to seven disciples), Mat-
> thew 28:1–10 (The resurrection of Jesus) and Matthew 28:16–20
> (The commissioning of the disciples).

What shall I return to the Lord
for all his bounty to me?
I will lift up the cup of salvation
and call on the name of the Lord,
will pay my vows to the Lord
in the presence of all his people.
Precious in the sight of the Lord
is the death of his faithful ones.
O Lord, I am your servant;
I am your servant, the child of your serving girl.
You have loosed my bonds.
I will offer to you a thanksgiving sacrifice
 and call on the name of the Lord.
I will pay my vows to the Lord
in the presence of all his people,
in the courts of the house of the Lord,
in your midst, O Jerusalem.
Praise the Lord!

Sung Refrain

Final Prayer and Blessing

VOICE 1:
We pray for the salvation of every soul
In the present, past, and future.
Deliver us from the idols that enslave us
And which keep us from you,
Idols of self, wealth, and power.
Deliver us from the hell that is reality without you

So that we may watch the seeds of heaven
Now taking root among us grow.
And may our church seek salvation for all
In life as in death,
The cry of both body and spirit.

We pray for the comfort of our kind
And of every creature, living, and dead,
For the balm that soothes the earth
And all its troubles.
And as our salvation depends on one another
We pray for the building of just societies
That will liberate the weak
Those who have too little
And those who have too much,
And all those preoccupied with survival
To pursue the things of the spirit
So we may all have the privilege of growing in love,
Joy, peace, patience and kindness,
In generosity, faithfulness, gentleness and self-control.
Have us raise one another up
Both in body and in soul
Reaching far beyond the merely personal
Toward a corporate salvation,
So we might enter heaven as one.

Voice 2:
In salvation we are moved
From captivity to freedom,
To the goodness that lies beyond
Our wildest imaginings,
To the resurrection life.

God here, God there, God everywhere,
Send us out in faith and hope
And bring us in with certainty and love.

FIVE

Divine Glory

The following *Liturgy of Divine Glory* celebrates the immanence of the divine in creation and the wonder and awe that the natural world, of which we are a part, so readily inspires. It seeks to facilitate a movement toward greater understanding and appreciation of the revelation of God in creation and the mutual dependence of all life on earth which must be respected if we are to secure our future on the planet. This service is a litany of thankfulness for all the delights, the grandeur, and the exquisite beauty of the world that has been given for the enjoyment of all living things.

The *Liturgy of Divine Glory* affirms the importance of the Holy Spirit's work in the natural world and through the events of life and history. It makes use of a theology in which God is both transcendent and immanent: God above, God the Incarnation, and God of Spirit, permeating all the cosmos. It puts in perspective the smallness of human beings in contrast with the greatness of creation, with its many worlds that we still know so little about, some of which are located on our own planet, deep inside the earth or under the seas.

This liturgy assumes natural revelation is akin rather than subordinate to revelation through religious tradition, scriptures, or through the Incarnation, while cautioning the worshiper against an overemphasis on divine immanence that leads to idolatry. Such an overemphasis has in the past been used by Christians and the church to justify their collusion in social engineering, eugenics, ethnic and social cleansing, and genocide, based on humanistic interpretations of the mechanisms of the natural world such as "social Darwinism." Rather, this liturgy aims to demonstrate how natural revelation should lift our aspirations to whatever is true, noble, right, pure, lovely, admirable, excellent, and praiseworthy (Phil. 4:8–9).

Secular culture and pragmatism have shaped the church through-out its history far more than many would care to admit. Indeed, the boundaries between the sacred and secular were once far from clear. However, even among today's pious who are so keen to separate the godly from the worldly, there has been no decline in their pragma-tism or materialism with regard to their lifestyles, or their modes of thinking when it comes to career and political ambitions. On the con-trary, they often exhibit best that worldliness they claim to so despise in their material greed and religious pride, rather like the Pharisees of Jesus' day.

Jesus spent his time in the world with tax collectors and sinners. These were the company he preferred, and he refused to condemn them; rather, he condemned the falsely pious and hypocritical. For anyone who claims to follow Jesus as an incarnation of God, it is of central importance that God be understood to be manifest in and through the world and its natural processes, since it was in Jesus that the divine became immanent in human flesh and demonstrated a great love of God for the world.

There is a kind of Christianity which, without being superstitious, speaks of angels or angelic beings and their presence all around us. It is an imaginative reenchantment of the world which reflects and cel-ebrates our admiration of the beauty of nature, which still has for us some mysterious and "magical" qualities, even for the most scientific among us. This is because our minds are too small to comprehend the whole of it at once, and we find ourselves won over by the impressions of great beauty and complexity such things as a vast landscape or intri-cate life-form can leave us with.

Angelic and other spiritual beings are a metaphorical way of describing God's agency in our immediate surroundings and the vis-ible world—those meanings we might subjectively perceive in nature at a particular time or in a particular place but which we would not be able to articulate in language in any literal way. They are also a way of acknowledging the feeling of God's near presence that can be as real to us as anything else. This liturgy makes reference to the angelic in this undogmatic and creative way, with the view that even though the world as perceived by the scientist and naturalist is of astonishing beauty in itself, the personification of its wonders is a natural, and in this case harmless, human device for engaging more fully with it. And our fuller engagement with nature, as I mentioned earlier in this book, could be key to giving us sufficient awareness and motivation to protect and nurture our environment, thus saving our species and our planet from the devastation that threatens it.

In preparation for this service it might be helpful to collect and display drawings, paintings, or poems on the subject of nature so that people can read them before and after the service. A haiku, for example, can capture succinctly a moment of natural revelation:

> I came across them
> A burst of woodland flowers
> In red autumn cold

It would be good if this liturgy were to inspire an outpouring of creativity in anticipation of the services in which it will be used. There can be few limits to the aesthetic indulgence and sumptuousness of a service of divine glory!

The reason why nature inspires, calms, and heals us as it does is partly because of its repetitive, fractal patterns, which are complex, familiar, and pleasing to the eye at any scale or distance you might be from the object of your gaze. Snowflakes are usually given as a good example of this complexity and variation. The white noise of wind and rain also has a soothing effect, as does fresh air because it has more negative ions and traces of ozone which give it its freshness and help to improve mood.

Watching other creatures contentedly going about their business is also calming. It contrasts with our tendency to overcomplicate things in our minds rather than simply observe them as they are in the present, and we cannot help but be won over and amused by their charming furry, scaly, and feathery forms, individual characters and eccentric movements. Though the sensitive might perceive in nature a tragic beauty, fleeting and fragile, always vulnerable and painfully close to decay and death, this reality is overwhelmed by the constant and triumphant rhythms of renewal and rebirth as every atom is recycled and springs to life again in new forms. These are just some of the physical facilitators of those spiritual experiences of interconnectedness or oneness and universal harmony that occur when we are outdoors and which make the natural world our most effective temple or church.

We are in every way made for this temple of nature that points to God, however much we might think we have adapted to an urban, indoor, and artificial existence. We simply cannot find our peace and well-being without it, which is perhaps the most compelling reason why its protection should be our priority.

THE LITURGY OF DIVINE GLORY

A central table could display images or objects brought by the participating individuals which remind them of God.

Sung Refrain

Welcome

VOICE 1:
Come with awe!

VOICE 2:
Come with wonder!

VOICES 1 AND 2:
Come with praise!

VOICE 1:
Roaring wave, and gentle dove,
God of splendor, God of love,

All:
God of paradise,
God of flesh,

God of all-pervading Spirit,
We open our eyes
And behold your glory!

Leaders light incense sticks and candles on the central table
as an offering to God.

Pauses should be employed between each voice entry below so that verses can be pondered for a moment. Where the word "silence" is written, a slightly longer pause should be observed.

Poem:
An Unending Hymn to God

VOICE 1:
You are love, O God,
The warmth in the midst of us,
The hopes that rise with the morning sun,
The calm that falls with the night.

VOICE 2:
You are the strength in human kindness,
The spirit of compassion that moves us,
The truth that unveils us.

VOICE 1:
You are vision,
Our glimpses of heaven,
Our moments of delight,
The triumph of the good.

VOICE 2:
You are courage,
To trust in a savior who walks beside,
Who will carry us through the valley of sorrows
To the summit where angels tread.

VOICE 1:
You are wisdom, O God,
The learning that humbles,
The knowing that we do not know,
That love which confounds our judgments.

VOICE 2:
You write in the shifting sands of our hearts
A verse of integrity.

VOICE 1:
You are the generosity that floods our senses
With unending creation,
A world of life that's constantly renewed,
The infinite that never wearies.

VOICE 2:
You are the noble, the right, the pure, and the lovely,
Clothed in the universe,
Perfected in the Incarnation
To be crowned by a redeemed humanity.

VOICE 1:
You are the admirable and the praiseworthy,
The beauty for contemplation,
The art for expression
The genius for excellence.

VOICE 2:
You are the untamed one, O God,
Who breaks free from our minds
And shatters our illusions,
The wild goose never captured,
The indeterminable flight of the spirit. . . .

Silence

VOICE 1:
For all you are,

We thank you.

***An Unending Hymn to God,* continued on p. 135**

Still-Speaking Parable:
The Secret Life of an Oak

VOICE 3:

As the sun gains height in the sky and turns to gold, there is a stirring in the forest, a crescendo of rustling, chattering, scuttling, and fluttering, the shrill melodies of tiny joyful throats and the rush of a thawing stream. I begin to awake from a long and silent slumber, from beneath a thick crust of gray-furrowed and deeply ridged bark, stretching out my withered branches toward the light, their tips growing tender with life. These sturdy limbs adorn themselves in the rich green leaves of my distinction, with edges notched and deeply lobed. They shelter a growing community of the furred and feathered, tireless parents, making nests for their young, and those escaping the rain. They set the stage at dawn for the dance of courting couples, and at dusk for the silver moon. As fresh leaves continue to unfurl, male and female flower buds expand in the rising warmth. The males droop in their downy clusters, releasing their pollen into the breeze and falling softly to the ground to form a bed of yellow worms.

The air begins now to shimmer with heat and humidity, and I watch as people begin to seek the shadow of my broad leaves and dense branches. I oblige them, of course, as I do in so many ways. I am a favorite in their parks and gardens for my shade, and my wood, hard and strong, is used by carpenters to make furniture, flooring, siding, fencing, and firewood for their homes. I am used in barrels for distilling, imparting my unique woody flavors to their wines and liquors. For centuries they have used my wood for building their ships, trusting me to carry them safely over the oceans. Without me they would not have survived the winters, let alone built their civilizations, but I wonder, do they know it?

There is now a distinct chill in the air and a hardening of the ground. The wind-blown pollen that alighted on adjacent female flowers has done its work, and each now blooms with an acorn. Creatures large and small such as squirrels, birds, deer, and bears gather around me for a period of great feasting, squabbling, and scurrying. The humans start to visit me once more, not this time for shelter but in anticipation of my crowning glory, my display in defiance of the fall: exceptional hues of yellow, orange, and red. My acorns drop heavily to the ground close by, and I, a proud parent once more, watch over them and wish them well. Animals busy themselves scattering them after they have eaten their fill, and the occasional acorn overlooked, or buried and forgotten by a rodent hoarder finds itself placed some distance from me, primed to sprout and grow.

Others have a more adventurous start, falling into stream or river, carried far away to some distant land where I will never see them rise out of the earth. Each acorn is laden with the hope of regaining a little ground, so much of which we have lost since our first generations and the age of the great forests.

The sun begins now to withdraw prematurely over the brow of the hill, leaving only the remnant of its thin white light, still penetrating the mass of foliage. The ground is growing hard and cold but I am no longer afraid of the coming gloom, for I was born many years ago to the sound of sirens and bombers overhead, a tiny sapling untouched by the war, a mere stone's throw from the mighty tree that gave me life. And life I have in abundance, for longer than you will ever know, indeed, for hundreds of years I may stand here tall and unashamed if I am left undisturbed by humanity.

Indeed, the oldest of my kind, no less than a thousand years old, still stands in defiance of hurricane and chainsaw. Some of you have taken us to heart as the emblem of your state or nation, in admiration of our strength and longevity. Others teach their children of the mutual dependence of all life on earth, planting again where they have cut down, and here lies our hope for the future.

Even I, however, must come to an end, for rot and disease and the elements do not weary, while I will not always have the energy or the will to overcome them. But when that time comes, I will crumble once more into earth; the muddy womb that will nourish another into life as it so nourished me and sustained me all my years. And everything of which I am composed will find its place in the life of plant and animal in this dear corner over which I once reigned. A few of my acorns, fallen, washed or carried away, will survive the hazards of the hungry nibbler, the violent assault of insects and the trampling of feet. Each will send down its taproot, send up its shoot, and begin its life as a young seedling. Some, as I did, will break bravely into light beyond the grasses, creepers, and shrubs, growing broad and magnificent, and towering over the landscape once again.

Silent Communion

Bread is broken and wine poured by a leader in silence. The bread and wine can then be passed from one worshiper to another until all who wish to take part have eaten and drunk.

> The bread and wine should be of especially good quality, reflecting the generosity of God. Spreads, dips, and so on can be used if necessary, or cake may be used instead of bread.

An Unending Hymn to God, continued from p. 132

VOICE 4:
You, O God, are the seen and unseen,
The known and the unknown,
The cosmos and beyond.

VOICE 5:
You are the angel in the storm and at our back,
The presence of the other in our solitude.

VOICE 4:
You are the king and queen of peoples
For none can rival the Poet of Life,
Neither monarch nor dictator,
Neither government nor authority of any kind
Can stand in the stead of God.

VOICE 5:
You, Divine Courage, are the peaceful revolt
And the fall of tyrannies,
Freeing the slave and reviving the thirsty,
Bringing the prisoners their reprieve.

VOICE 4:
You are always the better and the more,
The transcendence that intervenes
To save us from ourselves.
Yet you are also the immanence
In our conscience and moral sense
And in the natural order of cooperation and dependence.

VOICE 5:
You are the worldly and otherworldly good
With whom we seek oneness
And the ecstasy it brings,
The encounter with God in the personhood of Christ
Or the kindness of another.

VOICE 4:
You are the consecrated heart, filled with spirit,
And the contrite heart, filled with grace.

VOICE 5:
You are the divine image
Seen in the work of our hands
And heard in the song on our lips.

VOICE 4:
You are the talent, with which we worship,
Our renaissance and our enlightenment,
The outpouring of energy from within us.

VOICE 5:
You are the growth of animal and plant,
The gentleness that brings reflection and measure,
The forcefulness that breaks through to light.

VOICE 4:
You are the feminine and the masculine
And the bonding of the two,
The spontaneity of affection
And the arousal of unconditional love.

Voice 5:

You are the nurturer of infants
And a counsel to the young,
The one who always hears, always understands
And in listening alone responds.

Voice 4:

You are the tears of reunion joy,
The encouragement of a friend,
The exuberant and carefree play
Of the young of every kind.

Voice 5:

You, O God, are the stable by the inn
And a billet on the way,
The artlessness within the loving home,
The uninhibited embrace. . . .

Silence

Voice 1:

For all you are,

We thank you.

An Unending Hymn to God, continued on p. 139

Meditation on Scripture

Voice 6:

Exodus 3:1–15

Moses was keeping the flock of his father-in-law Jethro, the priest of Midian; he led his flock beyond the wilderness, and came to Horeb, the mountain of God. There the angel of the Lord appeared to him in a flame of fire out of a bush; he looked, and the bush was blazing, yet it was not consumed. Then Moses said, "I must turn aside and look at this great sight, and see why the bush is not burned up." When the Lord saw that he had turned aside to see, God called to him out of the bush, "Moses, Moses!" And he said, "Here I am." Then he said, "Come no closer! Remove the sandals from your feet, for the place on which you are standing is holy ground." He said further, "I am the God of your father, the God of Abraham, the God of Isaac, and the God of Jacob." And Moses hid his face, for he was afraid to look at God.

Then the Lord said, "I have observed the misery of my people who are in Egypt; I have heard their cry on account of their taskmasters. I know their sufferings, and I have come down to deliver them from the Egyptians, and to bring them up out of that land to a good and broad land, a land flowing with milk and honey, to the country of the Canaanites, the Hittites, the Amorites, the Perizzites, the Hivites, and the Jebusites. The cry of the Israelites has now come to me; I have also seen how the Egyptians oppress them. So come, I will send you to Pharaoh to bring my people, the Israelites, out of Egypt." But Moses said to God, "Who am I that I should go to Pharaoh, and bring the Israelites out of Egypt?" He said, "I will be with you; and this shall be the sign for you that it is I who sent you: when you have brought the people out of Egypt, you shall worship God on this mountain."

But Moses said to God, "If I come to the Israelites and say to them, 'The God of your ancestors has sent me to you,' and they ask me, 'What is his name?' what shall I say to them?" God said to Moses, "I am who I am." He said further, "Thus you shall say to the Israelites, 'I am has sent me to you.'" God also said to Moses, "Thus you shall say to the Israelites, 'The Lord, the God of your ancestors, the God of Abraham, the God of Isaac, and the God of Jacob, has sent me to you': This is my name for ever, and this my title for all generations."

Invitation

As the music is playing, you are invited to receive an anointing with aromatic oil from one of the leaders as a sign of the extravagant generosity of God, which we should emulate, and an affirmation of the pleasure that we are to take in the world God has given us.

The words "All the blessings of God are yours" can be used for the anointing.

An Unending Hymn to God, **continued from p. 137**

VOICE 7:
You, O God, are ripples of laughter in the air,
The swaying of ducks on a lake,
The teaming whirlpool eyes of another
Whose depths you alone can scale.

VOICE 8:
You are the voice that reaches unclaimed peaks,
The thundering falls of water,
And the countless suns and stars above,
Stealing the night and crowning the day.

VOICE 7:
You are the crescent of moonlight
That shimmers in my dark fields,
Reeling in the soul to pastel skies and swirling cloud.

VOICE 8:
You are the dusty beauty of desert and dune,
And your scent is the mist of gardens, dressed in the monsoon rain.
Yours are the rays that weave gold our scattered bales of hay,
The tender lips that brush softly, like fox cubs in the night.

VOICE 7:
You are the charmed one,
Fey as a whispering glen of dew-laden moss
With words that quicken shrouded minds
So they strike in pitch once more.

VOICE 8:
You are the amazon heart
Aglow with every hue
And the humor of nature's multitude,
Of the eccentric and bizarre,
Your thoughts so close
They stir the butterflies' wings to beat
As you watch and smile over great and small.

Bible texts for use in the Meditations on Scripture include Mark
14:3–9 (The anointing at Bethany), John 2:1–11 (The wedding at
Cana), or the accounts of the Transfiguration in Matthew 17:1–9,
Mark 9:2–8, and Luke 9:8–36.

VOICE 7:

You are courage to trek the wilds and ride the brooding seas,
To launch high into sky and space knowing you are also there,
For your love is sure as the sun to rise and warm the soils of earth,
Following each upon their way around every twist and turn.

VOICE 8:

You are a lofty canopy where orchid secrets rest unfurled,
The regal heights of a woodland's many-shaded green
And a jewel on nature's sovereign brow,
The marvelous reenchantment of modernity.

VOICE 7:

You are the catch that cheers the weather-beaten face
When sailing boats lie silent, wilting in the bay,
The sense of pride as the final stone is placed
When the task was strenuous and plagued with thorns.

VOICE 8:

You are the one who straightens the gale-bent reed
And raises the head of the mocked and scorned,
The one who grasps the pieces of a broken heart
And holds them in place till they beat again.

VOICE 7:

You, O God, are a spread of flowers
On the forest floor,
The sapling and the ancient tree,
The hearth and the wilderness. . . .

Silence

VOICE 1:
For all you are,

We thank you.

VOICE 2:
For all you are,

We sing your glory.

VOICES 1 AND 2:
For all you are,
We give our lives with gladness.

Sung Refrain

SIX

Justice and Peace

Both corporate healing and a coordinated practice of compassion are needed to secure the two outcomes by which the realm of God can be recognized: a state of justice and peace. Our concern should be healing on a national and international level as well as on the regional, local, and individual. It should also be the protection of the world's most vulnerable, those who suffer violence and exploitation due to corruption among those in power or the inadequacies of law and governance, and those who suffer because of widespread ignorance or moral degeneration and the persistence of cultural institutions that perpetuate cruel and degrading practices down the generations. Compassion must lead to healing in these areas by means of activism, fundraising, campaigning, and advocacy. It cannot shy away from politics if it is at all serious or sincere.

The most widespread and conspicuous injustice is the enormous and still-widening disparities in wealth both within and between nations, in which a privileged few, usually the top one or two percent of the population, own and control almost all the world's wealth and resources. It is the injustice of poverty and the prevalence of greed which leads to so many other evils, including appalling abuses of human rights and the denial of rights for the rest of creation. The *Liturgy of Justice and Peace* reminds us that a constant and active concern for the poor, the vulnerable, and the natural world is not an optional extra for those of the Christian faith but is in fact the very essence of the faith. The message of Jesus was groundbreaking in that it was a message of good news and liberation primarily for the poor, addressed to them directly by one among their own number, and a message which the poor were given the responsibility to promote.

Christianity has always been at its noblest and its least corrupt when it has been the driving force of nonviolent social revolution

143

and the liberation of the oppressed, and when it has helped to create societies where human rights and equality are enshrined in law and where the vast majority have access to the essential opportunities of education and a minimum standard of living whereby they can make of themselves whatever their talents allow.

These are societies where upward mobility is achieved by creating widespread opportunity and rewarding merit, the ingenuity and hard work that leads to excellence, while inherited money, class-based privileges, and family connections are not the main factors determining an individual's success or failure. In our time there is a stark choice for Christianity. It will either sink into a fundamentalist individualism that encourages the insularity and self-centeredness that leads to materialism and nepotism (its churches becoming a beleaguered minority, rightly alienated by the rest of society), or, it will mature in new and exciting ways, flourishing once more as the energy and inspiration for the liberation and enlightenment of "the least of these" (Matt. 25:40).

The *Liturgy of Justice and Peace* reminds us of our responsibility to take our part in the political process rather than sit back and blame or even demonize our leaders when they do wrong or make the mistakes inevitable for human beings. Those in leadership often have a thankless task, where whatever action they take, some will benefit unappreciatively, and others will feel aggrieved and make sure everyone knows about it. There is a lack of willingness to get one's hands dirty on the part of many churches, caused by fear of bad press should they get it wrong and on account of a false pride which wants to maintain the moral high ground. This can be contrasted with the overeagerness of some fundamentalist Christians to get their hands as dirty as possible in politics and the media but not in a good way! The churches which abstain, however, allow others to take the risks and responsibility and therefore the praise or blame that results from taking necessary and difficult decisions. Christian leaders and churches that are always shy of controversy not only confirm their own ineffectual and irrelevant status in the eyes of the world, but will also awake one day to discover that the moral high ground was annexed with ease a long time ago, by other not-for-profit secular charitable and alternative faith-based organizations. It is necessary to note that the percentages of people in many Western democracies who actually vote, let alone engage in politics in other ways, are shamefully small, in spite of their greater responsibility for the wealth divide and environmental damage, a situation which must surely change especially where Christian communities are concerned if they are to continue to claim to be true disciples of Jesus.

Many parts of the world are seeing the spread of what is known as the "prosperity gospel," or the message that the reason and reward for believing in the Christian God is that you will be rich and successful. Usually you are also obliged to join the church spreading that message, which then persuades you to give regular offerings which the preachers claim will return to you twice over or even tenfold from the hand of God if you are loyal to him. Of course the preachers of this message will often siphon off most of the money in a handsome salary for themselves and by more covert means.

It is true that the principles of hard work and honest dealings that are integral to the Christian way do reap material rewards and have often in history and in modern times led to social mobility and the eventual rise of Christian communities to the upper echelons of the societies they are in. There is nothing innately wrong with this, although wealth among Christians, as among any other group, does always tend to lead to a more materialistic culture that is less centered and dependent on God, however earnestly it started out.

It is after all "easier for a camel to go through the eye of a needle than for someone who is rich to enter the kingdom of God" (Matt. 19:24). We all know, of course, that the message of Jesus had a lot to do with the honest and generous use of money but nothing to do with voraciously seeking more of it than we require for a good and full life, let alone making the gain of riches the chief vision and end of faith. Jesus did champion freedom and better lives for the poor and outcast, and this necessarily involves the material gain for all that comes with material justice. However, Jesus was always clear that salvation and true contentment are to be found not only in bread and water, in matter, though God knows we both need and enjoy these things, but also in spiritual food and drink for the soul (John 4:10, 13–14). As I have said before, in true religion, material (or physical) salvation and spiritual (or moral) salvation cannot be separated.

In Jesus' economy there was quite enough money and other resources to go around if only people were willing to share them, so that everyone, rather than merely an acquisitive few, could enjoy the best of what God's creation has to offer. Jesus knew that only profound spiritual or inward changes in character would allow us to achieve fair distribution and to distinguish between what fulfills a need (and what might be fair to take for additional enjoyment) and what spoils us and harms others. Though it was impossible with humankind, he believed this economy both possible and imminent with God's help. His economy seems unrealistic, and history tells that human greed has always triumphed within even the most ardent of socialist agendas, let alone within unrestrained capitalist systems, however philanthropic a few individuals are purported to be. However, it seems still the stubborn duty of the Christian to hold on to at least some of the idealism of Christ in the hope that humanity will one day build a fairer social order for all. The unprecedented scale and interrelatedness of the environmental and human crises of our times may compel us yet as a species to heed some of the simple wisdom and goodness of that still-speaking Galilean.

THE LITURGY OF
JUSTICE AND PEACE

Worshipers could bring with them to this service a small item representing a justice or peace cause with which they have a connection. These can be placed on a central table as a focus for contemplation and as a gesture of solidarity with a vulnerable group of people, animals, or a threatened environment.

Sung Refrain

Welcome

VOICE 1:
Advocates, peacemakers,
Those who seek justice
And all who support them,
Let us pray in confidence
And inspire to action,
Living out our faith
As the people of the way,
Lighting that way
For younger generations
And all who have given up hope.

**We come together
In prayer and reflection
To consider the plight of the earth,
Of humanity and all living things,
To remember in solemnity,
To consider in kindness,
And to encourage one another
In the finding of solutions,
In the task of applying them
And in the will to work together
To carry them through.**

A poem on the subject of justice and peace can be read as a creative and poignant way of conveying a message. The poem below is one I wrote as if from the pepective of the most vulnerable people of the earth.

Voice 2:
Poem:
A Cry in the Land

Remember me, when the floods come
And the hurricane strips us bare,
When the torrent sweeps away our babes
And when I'm no longer fair.

Remember me, when the looters come
And the thieves take more than gold,
When the streets are painted with our blood
And the children bought and sold.

Remember me, when the skies run dark
And the wild beasts groan with hunger,
When we're savages at war with all
With fury, fire, and thunder.

Remember me, when the streams are dry
But the seas consume the land,
When the pregnant yearn to miscarry
Moving on through the bitter sand.

Remember me when terror strikes
And drains my heart of blood,
When even kin, turned on their own,
Dig grave-pits in the mud.

Remember me, when in distant lands
The cries of the fat are stronger,
For the same faces here in line
Have waited, mute and longer.

Remember me, when the pain is hot
And the strewn corpses cold,
When the ruins are overgrown with years
And our story's seldom told.

Remember me, my Savior love,
As you pass by those ears of corn.
Why not return in our forgotten time
On the crest of a breaking dawn?

You can't forget what once we knew,
What once was human-faced.
Or the natural world that gave us birth
Once paradise-laced.

Still-Speaking Parable:
The Pacifist and the Soldier

> This can be read by a narrator or by two people acting the parts of
> soldier and pacifist.

VOICE 3:

"So tell me soldier, what exactly are you fighting for?" asked the pacifist facetiously.

"For queen and country," replied the soldier without hesitation.

"But why?" continued the pacifist.

"For loyalty, for patriotism. . . . "

"But who is this queen to you, that she deserves your loyalty?" interrupted the pacifist, "and this land that it so deserves your love?"

"The queen and government protect our human rights and constitute our democracy," said the soldier. "They secure our freedoms and our equality under law. And the land, well, it is the place that gave me birth and nurtured me. It is in my blood—the home of those I love, my home."

"But what kind of share do you and those you love have in this freedom and land? Are you not really fighting to defend the property and privileges of the rich and indeed secure their further interests overseas that they might grow richer?" retorted the pacifist.

"It is true," said the soldier, "that I risk more in the fighting, and gain least when the spoils are divided, but nonetheless I do gain. I gain more of freedom and wealth than would be my lot under another kind of system, one that would soon take its place if it could. It would no doubt be some regime of tyranny and coercion such as most of the world's people have to suffer. War may be a capitalist conspiracy in part, one that largely benefits the few, but surely it is also a necessary evil for the sake of all?"

"So," said the pacifist, who now looked at the soldier with a perplexed expression, "you consider the risk worthwhile, though it may be greater than that of your 'superiors,' though it may cost you your life, and for such a small piece of the pie?"

"Sometimes," said the soldier, looking downward wearily. "Other times I only want to get the job done so I can pay the bills and come home. I have been long enough in the field to know there is no glamor to be found in war, only mud and filth, scorching heat or bitter cold, and the pathetic cries of the wounded and dying."

"So they've made you a slave to your wages. I suppose there's no alternative work for you," said the pacifist, angry once more.

"It is true that there's a shortage of work," the soldier conceded, "especially employment for the young and inexperienced and those who are not suited to the library or the office. I, however, wasn't forced to be here. I could have looked for other work, perhaps surviving on handouts from charity or government until I found it, but I chose to fight for my country and all it stands for, a decision of which I am sometimes proud and sometimes ashamed. But it is far better in my view than the menial and mind-numbing work that is the fate of most civilians, since they contribute mostly to the bank balances of wealthy owners and managers and gain comparatively very little for their own families and wider society."

"You are certainly brave," said the pacifist, "and I'm grateful for your part in keeping evil regimes and the greed of despots from our shores. It is also admirable that you risk so much to defend even the scraps that are left over for the likes of us once our own nation's gluttons have had their fill. But there must be better ways to achieve these ends than war, and to secure a far better deal for the majority. After all, war is surely an evil to match the threat of tyranny."

"There are other ways," said the soldier resolutely. "There is the way of forgiveness and reconciliation for the burying of past wrongs. There is the way of cooperation by which we could distribute the world's resources more fairly. There is the way of patient diplomacy and dialogue. There are these ways," said the soldier, looking intently into the eyes of his questioner. "But now I must ask you a question. If these ways are so much better, why are so very few willing to walk in them?"

Prayers for Victims of Injustice and Violence

VOICE 4:
We lay before you, O God,
All the pain and suffering that continues
Both in our midst
And in places far away.
Beyond the power of words
Is the healing that is needed.
So we pray with the spirit:
For those devastated by conflict,
For the victims of violent assault and rape,
For children forced to bear arms,
For those exploited and trafficked for sex,
For women and children denied their rights
And left unprotected by government and the law,
For victims of domestic abuse,
For those stricken by natural disasters,
By earthquakes, hurricanes, and floods
And their aftermath of disease and homelessness,
For wild, domestic, and farm animals
Treated with cruelty and neglect.
For Christian communities in minority situations,
Other ethnic and religious minorities,
Homosexuals, bisexuals, and the disabled,
And all who are subject to discrimination,
Persecution, or censorship,

For prisoners and detainees,
For the poor and destitute,
For those with acute or long-term illnesses,
For the lost and missing and their families,
For the dead, the dying, and the bereaved,
Those mourning victims of murder, violence, and war ,
And those called to minister to them.
We continue to remember our armed forces
And all those who risk their lives
To defend the lives of the rest of us
And preserve our freedom and security.
Give them in equal measure
Courage and mercy, strength and humility.

So great is this healing that is needed,
Healing of bodies and souls,
That for us it seems impossible.
But, our God of transformation,
You are the One who can achieve it.
So come to the side of the victims and the perpetrators of evil
With your goodness and your mercy
So that vicious cycles of revenge may be broken.
Call individuals and nations
To bold and costly steps
Toward repentance and compassion,
Forgiveness and reconciliation.
Strengthen our communities, God of hosts,
So that we might carry one another
Through the darkness of bewilderment and brokenness
And into the healing light of Christ.

Prayers for Environmental Justice

VOICE 5:
God, our creator and sustainer,
We thank you for all the wonders of the universe,
Especially the wonders of the earth.
It was not space that amazed the first astronauts

But the beauty of our blue planet
Seen from that great distance.
Help us, therefore,
To be responsible and active stewards
Who delight to conserve the environment,
The ecosystems you provide for our flourishing
And for the enjoyment of countless creatures
Of such fascinating complexity, variety, and intelligence.
Help us to insure their protection under law
And to cooperate with their human neighbors
For the benefit of all.
We pray also for endangered species
For animals abused and exploited for our use,
And all of life affected by our greed and pollution
And the loss of habitat and home.
Give us the determination
To use renewable resources and ethical products
And develop new technologies for clean energy
To bring an end to our part in climate change,
To alleviate its present consequences,
And to prevent future wars over water and food.

We pray for all those who seek knowledge
Of the universe and humanity
And those who contemplate our values and meaning,
Including scientists, mathematicians, philosophers, theologians,
Communities both religious and secular,
That they would travel with one another
On this exciting quest,
One that is, after all,
So essentially human.
May conflict give way to conversation,
Bigotry to understanding,
Cynicism to hope,
Hatred to love,
And fear to the courage that keeps on learning,

So that all the earth might thrive
In a deep and lasting peace.

Prayers for Social Justice

VOICE 6:
God of work and rest,
Of the hurried and the still,
Give us strength and motivation to complete the tasks
With which you have entrusted us.
May we work not simply for wage or employer
But for a shared purpose,
The completion of all that is useful to humankind
And brings glory to God,
Drawing heaven closer to the earth.
Give inspiration and new opportunities
To the unemployed
And those who find little fulfillment in their work,
For whom the breaking of day brings only sadness
And the sense of futility and failure,
That they might find their niche within the realm of God
As it germinates within urban and rural life,
That they might flourish as you intended
In peace and prosperity,
Finding dignity and comradeship among their colleagues,
Seeing the fruits of their effort, skill, and creativity
As you, O God of all beginnings,
Looked upon your own creations
And called them good.

We remember especially those millions
Who, alienated from the products of their labor,
Are exploited for the gain of the rich and powerful.
God, give us and those who lead us
The means to bring about more just societies,
The fairer distribution of resources and wealth,
Fairer trade and local trade,
And the means for growth and modernization

Which do not require
The sacrifice of the vulnerable
Nor the destruction of the earth.

In our increasingly urban reality
Where the world has become a unity
For which we are unprepared
And in many ways unfit,
Expand our hearts to encompass
Not just our own cities or towns
But all the world's peoples
Upon whom we have an impact
As we buy and sell, drink and eat.
Let us be mindful of the ways
In which we can prevent and alleviate
The suffering of those whose work
Sustains the fabric of our lives.
God, prepare us to make sacrifices
To take the action our faith demands,
Not only for the few
But to build a better future for us all.

God, make us aware and repentant of our corporate sins
Which have cast their long shadow over humankind,
For we are all responsible for the corporations
And systems that have outgrown us.
So bring before us, O God,
Our sins of omission and negligence
And the evils that have so often outwitted and deceived us,
Those that have entered our business models,
Our markets, social orders, and political processes.
Help us to reclaim the total morality that demands the whole of life,
Both public and private.
Keep us vigilant, God of peace,
So that our inventions and the products of our labor
Do not become a curse but remain a blessing.
Shield us from the greed that so often consumes us,

Hardening our hearts so that they turn away
From the pain of others.
Nurture in each of us
The compassion of Christ.

Help us, God of grace, where we live in comfort,
To be content with what we have
Without envy and covetousness,
For, God, you are a generous God
And there is nothing to be gained by grasping.
You have made it so that we would gain
Far more from giving than receiving.
So we give you all that we are,
Our innovative minds and industrious hands,
And ask that our lamps would not go out
Until all are fed and clothed,
Until the vulnerable see justice among the living.

Prayers for Our Leaders

VOICE 7:
Keeper of all life, we pray for our leaders.
Help them to put the good stewardship of national resources
Before political partisanship and greed.
May they lead us in the pursuit of economic justice,
That justice so passionately called for
By the prophets of the Old Testament
But which seems ever further from realization
In our modern times.
Now social change and advances in knowledge
Are more rapid than ever before.
May our leaders seek sustainability
Both here and overseas,
Insuring we and those who trade with us
Will know greater freedom and security
And improving the quality of life for all.

God of wisdom, be a guide to our leaders,

Those who bear the burden of many choices,
Decisions too great for humanity,
Where their every action or omission
Must please some and grieve others,
When the best course of action is unclear
And the outcomes known only to you.
Remind us often not to be complacent,
Leaving the work to others or the state,
But as children born for a realm of God,
Have us build ourselves that realm
In this our generation.

Invitation

While the music is playing, you are invited to light a candle and place it by one of the items on the central table as a gesture of prayer and solidarity.

VOICE 1:
We say together in words of Mary:

My soul magnifies the Lord,
And my spirit rejoices in my savior.
God looks with favor upon my humility,
And from henceforth all generations shall call me blessed.
The almighty works marvels for me,
One whose name is Holy,
Whose mercy endures from age to age.
Upon those who fear divine justice,
God has shown strength of arm,
Shattering the proud in the imagination of their hearts,
Casting the mighty from their thrones
And exalting the lowly.
God has filled the hungry with good things,
While the rich have been sent away empty.
The Lord receives my nation as a servant,
Remembering to be merciful
As was promised to our ancestors,

The children of God, forever.

Communion

VOICE 2:
Holy is our God,
Whose moral law is our highest goal.
To reach it with our passions
And in spite of them
Is our greatest desire.
We contemplate it day and night,
Striving for sophistication
In our pursuit of truth,
For a taste of every subtle shade
On the path to holiness,
Every drop of wisdom
We can contain.

VOICE 1:
But straining to be perfect
Proves a futile enterprise
Leading only to pride,
To self-righteousness and hypocrisy,
Instead we must embrace the uncertain and untamable
The flow and flux and paradox
With which all creatures contend.
We let ourselves drift out of sight of land
With the tide of trust in a higher wisdom,
Taking comfort in a moral law
Threefold in black, white, and gray,
And yet secure under the auspices of God.
For we cannot always do good,
Every action having its ripples
To the left and to the right.
Yet we discern as we mature
Not only what is evil or saintly
But see the great swath of life that's in-between.

And open our minds to many a delicate balance
Slowing, restraining, humbling our judgments.
We learn too that the world will show us benevolence
And sometimes hostility,
But mostly a quiet and sweet indifference,
For such is the state of things.

VOICE 2:
But as creatures of purpose
Orientated in work and creative ambition
Always toward an end or a goal,
We crave meaning,
A narrative that integrates
Every aspect of the self,
And the branches of our societies
We draw order out of chaos
For health and peace of mind
And will to express unrestrained
Our unique personalities,
Doing as we cannot help but do
While learning to steer the ship remotely
From the helm and not the bow
By developing the habits of virtue
That we might grow noble in character.

VOICE 1:
We cultivate humor to soothe the troubled heart,
As the sublime unites with the ridiculous,
The elegant with the absurd to save us.
But when all is noise and confusion
And the trail is overgrown
We call out to God:

Let me go with you, my counselor, my teacher,
For wherever you go I will follow you;
Wherever you live, I will live.
Your people will be my people,
And wherever you ask me to, I will go.

I will follow wherever you lead.

VOICE 2:
I will come to you, wherever you are,
Says the God of salvation in answer,
For wherever you go, I will go.
Your people will be my people,
And nothing shall separate us.
Whenever you need me, I will be with you.
Wherever you are, there I shall be.

VOICE 1:
So it is that Christians follow,
Not a prescribed law,
But the way of Jesus,
Who taught us to pray to God
As one would speak to a loving parent,
And he asked to be remembered in a simple meal
Around a common table,
The picture of sharing and companionship,
Openness and equality.
He welcomes us to the table,
Telling of the God who sits among us in friendship
With the greatest and least in the eyes of humanity,
But sisters and brothers in the eyes of God.

Raising and breaking the bread

This is the bread of our union,
Broken to reveal how the world may be fed.

Raising the cup of wine

This is the wine of our sustaining,
Poured for the quenching of every thirst.

The bread is passed around the group with the words:

The body of Christ, for the feeding of the world.

The wine is passed around the group with the words:

The blood of Christ, to satisfy your thirst.

A time of silence is kept.

Voice 1:
Let us offer up our lives in the service of God:

My all I give to make aright,
To speak for those in depth of night.
The close and distant I shall see,
And pray they too remember me.

Meditation on Scripture

Voice 8:
Matthew 25:34–40

Then the king will say to those at his right hand, "Come, you that are blessed by my Father, inherit the kingdom prepared for you from the foundation of the world; for I was hungry and you gave me food, I was thirsty and you gave me something to drink, I was a stranger and you welcomed me, I was naked and you gave me clothing, I was sick and you took care of me, I was in prison and you visited me." Then the righteous will answer him, "Lord, when was it that we saw you hungry and gave you food, or thirsty and gave you something to drink? And when was it that we saw you a stranger and welcomed you, or naked and gave you clothing? And when was it that we saw you sick or in prison and visited you?" And the king will answer them, "Truly I tell you, just as you did it to one of the least of these who are members of my family, you did it to me."

Final Prayer and Blessing

May the church seek justice
As integral to discipleship,
For we are called to join together
To resist evil with nonviolent protest
And constructive activism
To inspire strong commitments

To the earth and all its creatures,
Caring and cultivating,
Rebuilding our civilizations
In sustainable, compassionate ways.

**O God, make your presence known
In every nook and cranny of our urban life
That it might be transformed into that heavenly city
Where churches will have no need of walls,
For God will walk among us in the streets and in the gardens,
And peace and prosperity will reign.**

Sung Refrain

Bible texts for use in the Meditations on Scripture include Luke 4:18–19 with Isaiah 61 (Jesus' Gospel), Luke 18:1–8 (The widow and the unjust judge), John 15:18–21 (The world's hatred), Matthew 5:13–14 (Salt and light), Matthew 5:43–48 (Love for enemies), or James 2:14–26 (Faith without works is dead), and Matthew 19:16–26 (The rich young man). There are also many shorter passages and verses that could be combined with pauses in between, such as Proverbs 31:8–9 (Speaking up for those who cannot speak for themselves), 1 Corinthians 12:25–27 (When one suffers in the church, all suffer), Hebrews 13:3 (Remembering those in prison), Romans 12:15 (Weeping with those who weep) and John 15:18–21, Matthew 5:10 and 2 Timothy 3:12 (On suffering persecution), and so on.

SEVEN

Friendship

The *Liturgy of Friendship* explores the art of building relationships and community and helps to define the mission of the church. Friendship is essential for both personal and social development and the formation of church. It is not always easily mastered, however, and does not always obey the rules we might like to apply to it. It is a messy and often unpredictable business which requires quiet consideration and prayer.

Liturgies like this one can help to create an environment that nurtures and encourages friendship. Included in this liturgy are opportunities for celebrating the long service of older members of the group, the potential of young people, and prayers of commissioning for those embarking on a new stage or adventure in life. There is also a section focused on the oil that lubricates any successful community: confession, forgiveness, and reconciliation. As part of a liturgy which helps us to really value one another, the appreciation of long service gives special opportunity for acknowledgment and gratitude to be shown to older members of the group who have contributed a great deal to society or the local community and church. In a time when youth is almost worshiped and older people are marginalized and often unheard despite their increasing numbers, it is important for the church to rebuild respect and admiration for age and experience.

The liturgy explores further the importance of building community and shared life in an age of social networking, gaming, and an online virtual reality. Our bodies and brains have not evolved anywhere near as rapidly as our technologies, and we still require real companionship, daily interaction with others, and a sense of belonging to a physical place and community to maintain our psychological health and general well-being. If we cannot achieve this alongside our technological advances, our societies will continue to fragment until we will find ourselves rushing headlong into our own self-destruction as a civilization and even as a species.

Another art, the art of hospitality, is absolutely essential to shared life and the building of friendships, especially in these days when most families in the developed world are small and scattered and few of us know our neighbors. We must learn again how to enjoy the conviviality that was so natural to our ancestors, who were more at ease with one another, whether strangers or friends, than we are today. It will be the continued breakdown of our social units, the increasingly limited circles of real friendship (despite the long lists of pseudofriends people like to claim on Facebook), and our increasing reluctance (and deteriorating ability) to be hospitable which will lead to the demise of church, if not to the misery and ruin of all.

Friendship is by far the most effective means by which spiritual insights and benefits are spread. The numerical growth of the churches depends entirely upon the success of friendships which bring people into the community of faith for the long term. The loss of friendship and belonging, for whatever reason, is the most common cause of people leaving a faith community as they are driven to search for a place of belonging elsewhere. However, friendship is not a tool for proselytizing but a glorious end in itself.

The false or forced friendliness, or "love-bombing" methods of the fundamentalist churches, which prioritize a very narrow understanding of evangelism that seeks to convert people to their specific creed over genuine relationships and the building of community, suffer the greatest exodus once converts discover the shallow nature of their welcome.

The *Liturgy of Friendship* helps, in contrast, to lay the groundwork for a theology that nurtures real relationships based on honesty and straightforwardness, with the understanding that friendship, rather than creed, is the cement by which the city of God (another heavenly methaphor) will be held together. It is through friendship that we help one another to maintain the key spiritual disciplines of meeting together regularly as church, living in community, praying, and reading Christian literature. For these reasons, friendship is not just a means for mission, it *is* the mission of the church. Part of the mission of friendship and community building is helping others toward salvation in all its aspects, and this can be done by sharing one's own stories. These stories will of course always reflect one's own religious context. One can have no better way of sharing insights and experiences. However, it should be done not for the sake of conversions to one's own set of beliefs but in order to inspire others to lead a moral life for the good of all and to enable them to enjoy all the blessings of a faith in God.

This liturgy also explores our need and desire for the shared spiritual experiences of interconnectedness, or oneness with God and humanity and the whole created order, which friendships and community allow. It is these ecstatic and potent experiences which distinguish religious communities from philosophical ones. They tell of our need for one another, for community and shared life beyond any mere intellectual interaction or agreement.

This need includes but goes beyond our practical needs determined by our evolution, such as the need for collaborative specialization that enables us to concentrate on complex tasks without spend most of our time worrying about acquiring the basic materials for our survival. It goes beyond even our need to raise one another above subsistence so that we can have the time, energy, and privilege of considering spiritual things and realize our corporate salvation.

We crave a state of consciousness or awareness in communion with others in addition to these crucial aspects of community, a state of elation that can only be described in terms of the spiritual. This state can be achieved through quiet corporate meditation but is also achieved through singing with others and experiencing together the rhythms, melodies, and harmonies of music which play on our keenest emotions. The other needs that a community built on friendships fulfills are the need for a common memory, identity, and purpose, and a sense of belonging or home. These needs stir our desire for ceremonial or emblematic reminders of the things that we have in common. Our patriotism and services of remembrance often pick up upon this aching to be part of a greater narrative and family.

While the *Liturgy of Friendship* fleshes out a theology of healthy relationships and celebrates their capacity for communicating the awesome love of God, the opportunities for confession, forgiveness, and reconciliation address in practice the universal human experience of relationships turned sour, an all-too-common state of affairs for humanity. Central to the Christian message has always been the power of the Gospel, or good news, news of the extravagant forgiveness of God in spite of our continued vices, which breaks through our pride and stubbornness and unleashes our own ability to confess wrongdoing, to empathize, and to have compassion for one another's frail humanity.

This empowers us to work together and engage in dialogue in order to solve our differences with the hope of reconciliation. It is a thorny, humbling, and often painful business, because there is no cheap grace, at least none which would stand the test of time. Just as Jesus suffered, we may well suffer in what can be a long and arduous process of forgiveness or reconciliation and we may well have to make difficult sacrifices or concessions along the way. There is also the chance that efforts at reconciliation may prove impossible, perhaps for purely practical reasons (one party being unable to participate in the process because of distance, ill health, or because they die before the process can take place) or because one party flatly refuses to participate in the process or to admit their own guilt.

In some cases, one party may still be continuing in the destructive pattern of behavior that led to the initial grievance, making forgiveness difficult, as it would have to be constantly renewed. Reconciliation would be more difficult still. In these cases the only solution might be to remove oneself from the situation and company indefinitely, since this will at least allow one's own process of forgiveness and healing to proceed. Then one can live in hope that such people will one day become more self-aware, even remorseful, and eventually change their ways. This kind of situation is particularly painful (though very common) in families, and in this case, where people feel duty bound to remain connected, the person continually doing harm has to be carefully managed and kept at a suitable distance so as not to prevent the emotional healing and forgiveness on the part of the others.

It is very important that churches recognize these complex situations and do not talk simplistically and sentimentally about forgiveness and reconciliation, ignoring its practical complications and the very real need for aggrieved parties to have the space to heal before they can forgive. Those who have suffered because of another's anger, dishonesty, betrayal, or abuse, especially if the suffering was sustained for months or years, will need considerable time to heal that reflects the magnitude of what was done. They have every right, especially the victims of heinous crime, or their relatives, to take the months or years this demands without feeling pressured to seek reconciliation, or even to reach a point where they can say they have completely forgiven. It must be remembered that forgiveness is not the finding of some spurious means to make something that was wrong or unjust appear to be right or justifiable in one's own mind or that of others.

A related point to make is that an acceptance and inclusion, as far as possible, of all the different types of human personality and mind that exist is an important aspect of these liturgies, particularly the *Liturgy of Friendship*. Very specific formulations of religious beliefs, practices, and priorities, laid down in mission statements, creeds, laws, or unwritten or even unspoken but nonetheless binding conventions, are necessarily exclusive, because they presume that everyone can be a prophet, evangelist, speaker of tongues, or even that everyone can go down the same path in life, getting a middle-class education or job or getting married, for example.

The fact is that whatever type of spiritual life one champions, there will always be people who are not at all suited to it and those who are simply not capable of it. For this reason there have to be many different branches and expressions of Christian community and worship for the church universal to be truly inclusive. Reflection and contemplation are, relatively speaking, very inclusive practices and good for almost everyone to learn, even those who might initially consider themselves unsuited or incapable of them. However, there will always be a small number people who are not yet ready or willing to reflect deeply on their life and faith, and a few who are unable to do so. They must be included equally in the broader life of the church.

The *Liturgy of Friendship* provides a framework and means to facilitate the three processes of confession, forgiveness, and reconciliation in a more general way, avoiding the rather trite calls to an instant forgiveness that offends our sense of justice and is an impossible demand, but which unfortunately the church has often been guilty of making. It also explores the corporate nature of sin, since everything we do and say has an impact on the rest of humanity for both good and ill. We have jointly created systems, structures, and establishments which have become good or evil in themselves, and whose identity has been so far removed from our identity as individuals that we have lost sight of who is responsible for them.

It is important that we regain responsibility for our world, despite its complexity and its apparent escape from the means by which we once thought we could control it, while maintaining a balanced perspective on ourselves as both the guilty party and the innocent victim in it all. This way we can be kind to ourselves and avoid getting caught up in entirely futile cycles of self-loathing and guilt, while nonetheless actively pursuing change for the good both within our own homes and in the wider social, political, and business structures we have created. This liturgy moves away from the churches' obsession with individual sin, guilt, introspection, and shamefulness which has proven to be damaging for those who have bought into it and does not correspond to our experience of real life, including our own dual nature, in which we find both good and evil, rather than total depravity.

However, while the liturgies here acknowledge the good in humanity and creation, they are certainly not naïve about or attempting to trivialize the reality of evil. There are those who may not have experienced confrontation with something or someone who appears to be devoid of any glimmer of good, but for those who have it is so very unmistakable and unexplainable in any other terms than the evil, or even demonic or satanic. Of course, there are those who foolishly call what is good (or what is neither good nor bad) evil, through ignorance or carelessness with the use of the word, but there are also genuine cases in which people have experienced a dark place in their own soul, or met with a wicked dictator or other criminal mind, and seen something beyond ordinary vices and flaws.

Some people have been so shaken by the experience that it has precipitated a swift religious conversion as God is sought out as the saving antidote to such a presence. For even fervent atheists, it is sometimes a brush with evil that sends them running for the first time into the arms of a God who is suddenly very real to them also. For these reasons it is important that sin and wickedness be treated with the utmost seriousness and that we do not get into the habit of absolving ourselves and one another too easily. Having said this, we must not allow ourselves to go down the route that many modern churches have which gives far too much space, credence, and air time to devils and demons and dark forces.

This kind of superstition, which preaches more about Satan than about God, is spreading in many parts of the world and has had, when it has been allowed to run its course, appalling consequences, such as child abuse in the guise of supposed exorcisms. It is, however, of the utmost importance that we do not shy away from discussing controversial matters regarding how to address evil when it comes to running a fair justice system, including issues surrounding reformative and retributive methods of justice and the debate surrounding capital punishment.

We must look carefully to science and psychology to better understand what is going on in the brains of those who commit crimes and what potential there is and could be in the future for their reform, while also looking closely at the long-term effectiveness of the various punishments we use as deterrents for both the convicts in question and would-be criminals. We must look to ourselves and ask ourselves whether we can really take responsibility for ending the life of another in the name of justice. It is possible only to find optimal solutions to anti-social behavior with the information we presently have about the nature of human volition, solutions which respect all of life and prioritize compassion. Ideal solutions are sometimes impossible to obtain in practice or even to be conceived in theory with regard to the most difficult cases.

This liturgy explores some of the complexities of morality which we face as human beings. Morality is often about fulfilling our higher goals rather than our immediate desires, which requires us to master and overcome our passions. A very sophisticated morality is needed to get to the truth, since there are so many gray areas and three levels of morality: that which seems obviously good, that which seems

obviously bad, that which seems both good and bad (in close propor-
tions) or perhaps neither good nor bad. The category of things that are
both good and bad (or neutral) is by far the largest, and accounts for
the many gray areas.

Often, for example, it is impossible to do "good," because there
are so many things we need to do every day that we simply could not
keep conscious track of, let alone compute the weight of all the effects
all our actions have on others and the world. We would find it very
difficult, for example, to determine that absolutely everything we buy
is ethically produced. Some people steer clear of politics for this very
reason of moral complexity, because in politics one is forced to take
many public decisions, such as where to spend government money,
which means one is often forced to do one of a limited number of possible things, all of which will have positive consequences for some and
negative consequences for others. This of course is not a convincing
excuse for being apolitical. It should instead be an encouragement to
all of us to be more forgiving and supportive of those who do step up
to the challenge.

Despite moral complexity, however, it is as important now, as it
was in ancient times, to cultivate the cardinal virtues of prudence (the
ability to judge how best to act), justice (proper moderation between
self-interest and the rights and needs of others), temperance (restraint,
self-control, moderation, and abstention), and fortitude (courage,
endurance, forbearance, or the ability to confront fear, uncertainty,
or intimidation). They need to be practiced in community until they
become almost instinctual, an innate character, state of mind, or fixed
attitude of the heart, until the facets of our lives are integrated into
a seamless whole, and until we find our corporate holiness. Due to
the universality of human imperfection and indeed the deficiencies
throughout creation that have brought about its description as fallen,
and the fact that things are never wholly within our control, we will not
achieve this complete holiness in our lifetimes, though we may perhaps achieve it after death. We can only aspire to it and be thankful for
any minor developments in the direction of holiness within ourselves
and within the people around us.

THE LITURGY OF FRIENDSHIP

Sung Refrain

Welcome

VOICE 1:
We join together in worship
And come together in friendship,
Uniting in the peace of God,
For Christian life is community life,
Its fruit born of relationships
Whose nurturing and repair
Must be the constant practice
Of the children of God,
At the heart of our devotion
And our life together.

By our care for one another
We raise each other from the mire
And into the light of Christ,
The light of our salvation.

Prayer

VOICE 2:
As we begin to pray,
We deepen our awareness of the transcendent God,
The God beyond the senses and the finite mind,
The God who intervenes in our affairs
With compassion, to save us.

In prayer,
We broaden our awareness of the immanent God
Whose voice whispers in our consciences,
Who walks among us, incarnate,
Whose glory is revealed in the natural world.

This is the God we come to worship,
To pour out our devotion,
To offer our allegiance,

To acknowledge our dependence,
So we confess our weaknesses and wrongdoings
And seek deliverance from evil,
Evil which we have caused by our actions
And by our failures to act.
We turn away also
From harm done to us by others
So that we might forgive
Just as we are forgiven,
Freeing our hearts and theirs
From the heavy burden of bitterness and regret
And the spiraling destruction of vengeance.

We turn instead to a new dawn,
A time to make peace and strive for justice,
A time to engage in costly discipleship,
A time to build the realm of God.
We cultivate holiness in community,
The striving after God's perfection
In our interactions and exchanges,
For holiness is known by its works,
While piety so often deceives.
For we are unable always to do right,
Having sometimes to choose the lesser of evils
Or to tread one path among many
That are lined with rose and thorn.
For morality is black, white, and gray,
And much is neither good nor ill.

So help us God, in our dilemmas
And when we are tempted by evil
That we might do according to your love
And be according to your truth
The best that we are able.

Invitation to Confession

VOICE 1:
We accept God's invitation to confession:

I confess to God, the Author of Life
And to my witnesses here present
That there have been times
When I have acted and spoken
In ways that have caused harm to others
And harm to myself.
I confess to the God of new beginnings
And to my witnesses here present
That there have been times
When I have neglected to speak and to act
In ways that are compassionate and just.
I turn my back on these sins,
Sins of both action and omission,
And seek from God and humanity
Forgiveness and reconciliation
With all my heart.
God, inspect my character
And my inmost thoughts and intentions,
Shine your light upon them
That I might grow in self-awareness
And in the understanding of others,
That my motivations may be purified
By the indwelling of your spirit,
That I might become fairer and kinder
Toward others and toward myself.

Invitation to Forgiveness

We accept God's invitation to forgiveness:

As God lived among us and knew our frailty,
So we live among others
Knowing their frailty as they know ours.
We learn then to forgive as God has forgiven us,

Neither with cheap sentiment nor hollow words
But by humility,
Recognizing our humanity, seeing it in others,
And finding relief from resentment and hatred
By moving forward
And letting the past be in the past
Far from our present thought
And the wiles of the imagination.
Keep us then, God of peace
In mindfulness of the joy that is forgiveness
So that we may always
Seek it, grant it, and find it near.

Invitation to Reconciliation

We accept God's invitation to reconciliation:

We extend the hand of friendship
To those we have forgiven
And those who have forgiven us,
To all who are able to take hold of it,
Joining in conversation and understanding,
Going forward to cooperation and joint endeavor,
To friendship and to love.
We pray for those who continue to do harm,
Those for whom our forgiveness must come,
But with distance and parting,
Until the other has come to a place of understanding,
Knowing the harm they do
And seeking to turn away from it and start anew.
We also pray for those who cannot yet forgive,
Who are consumed by their anger and hurt.
God bring healing to their souls and set them free,
Free to love and live once more.

Invitation

As the music is playing, you are welcome to light a candle as a symbol of a private confession or the resolve to seek (or grant) forgiveness or to initiate reconciliation.

Proverbs of Friendship

The Proverbs can be read one per voice around the group.

1. There are many kinds of friendship, each with its own boundaries. The wise learn to respect those boundaries and adapt to people with different needs, strengths, and weaknesses.

2. The wise appreciate different types of mind, without ranking others in terms of a particular attribute or ability or considering them only in terms of their expediency.

3. The wise make an effort to forge friendships across divisions of race, religion, culture, and economic background, knowing these can bring the greatest rewards.

4. Good and lasting friendships require effort but yield so much more than they demand.

5. Lives shared without fear and suspicion, without disapproval and impatience, are the happiest of all. Therefore, the wise are honest in their dealings and are slow to judge others.

6. Those that cooperate for a greater good than the fulfillment of personal ambition are richly rewarded.

7. The wise cultivate emotional maturity as intelligence akin to any other. They exhibit neither emotional incontinence nor excessive restraint. Nor are they passive-aggressive, fearing disagreement or confrontation and speaking unkindly behind the backs of others. Instead, they take courage to stand firmly yet with humility for what they believe to be right.

8. The wise are content with and kind to themselves, while working nonetheless to improve their own characters. They learn to love themselves while trying hard to be better. They do not

expect or strive to be liked by everyone, knowing that to be an impossible task that would require falseness and the loss of all integrity.

9. The wise, while trying their utmost to be loyal and generous, expect to disappoint and to be disappointed, to hurt others at times and to be hurt, for no one is perfect. They are quick to be forgiving of the failings of both themselves and others.

10. The wise do not stereotype others, making hasty or unjustified assumptions. They take each person as they find them, with an attitude of learning rather than teaching, of openness rather than scrutiny.

11. The wise do not expect to be able to change others or solve all their problems. They understand they can help only those who desire to be helped. They do not compromise their health trying to assist those who are unwilling, or trying to meet the needs of too many at one time. They ensure they are well and able to give in quality as much as in quantity.

12. The wise make an effort to know and to entertain the lonely and the marginalized, discovering angels in the process.

13. The wise build community by nurturing an environment where both friendships and romances can seed and blossom, where every personality has its place. They know that successful communities are built on cooperation more than competition. They know that we must collaborate for collective success of which personal success is the by-product, and so they help one another to fulfill their potential. They strive to rid themselves of jealousy, knowing that it harms, most of all, those who are jealous.

14. Some people are incapable of normal friendship due to a deficiency in self- and social awareness. Others are not yet in a place where friendship is possible due to emotional damage and personality disorders. The wise pray for these people and show them kindness. They maintain healthy boundaries with

them so that they are not too great a burden on other members of the community.

15. The wise turn their weaknesses to strengths, challenging themselves socially as they do intellectually and physically, knowing that practice alone leads to perfection in being a good companion, playmate, conversationalist, host, counselor, and in all social matters as in everything else.

16. The wise do not substitute real friendships for social networking sites or reality television. They take the risks involved in meeting people face-to-face, knowing this will bring far greater rewards. They use new technologies only to enhance these real relationships.

17. The wise relate to all with warmth, friendliness, and respect. They do not assume another's romantic interest without hearing an expressed declaration. Nor do they stay silent or behave ambiguously when they take a romantic interest, but express it with the honesty and the humility that risks rejection. For they know that all will experience rejection in life, just as we will all experience welcome and love. The wise are straightforward in their romantic relationships as in every other area of life.

18. The wise are neither cold nor hostile out of pride or arrogance or out of fear of hurt. They know friendship and love are worth the pain they might bring and that a life of self-protection will easily be filled with as much suffering, if not more.

19. The wise are not afraid to fail. They know that one day they will succeed and that their previous failures will have helped them to develop the skills and character to do so.

20. The wise are slow to take offense and less needy of approval. They do not measure themselves against others but against the yardstick of Christ whom they follow. They are not resentful or envious of those who are more successful but rejoice in one another's blessings, so that what is good news for one becomes good news for all.

Meditation on Scripture

VOICE 3:

The Parable of the Prodigal and His Brother, Luke 15:11–32

Then Jesus said, "There was a man who had two sons. The younger of them said to his father, 'Father, give me the share of the property that will belong to me.' So he divided his property between them. A few days later the younger son gathered all he had and traveled to a distant country, and there he squandered his property in dissolute living. When he had spent everything, a severe famine took place throughout that country, and he began to be in need. So he went and hired himself out to one of the citizens of that country, who sent him to his fields to feed the pigs. He would gladly have filled himself with the pods that the pigs were eating; and no one gave him anything. But when he came to himself he said, 'How many of my father's hired hands have bread enough and to spare, but here I am dying of hunger! I will get up and go to my father, and I will say to him, "Father, I have sinned against heaven and before you; I am no longer worthy to be called your son; treat me like one of your hired hands."' So he set off and went to his father. But while he was still far off, his father saw him and was filled with compassion; he ran and put his arms around him and kissed him. Then the son said to him, 'Father, I have sinned against heaven and before you; I am no longer worthy to be called your son.' But the father said to his slaves, 'Quickly, bring out a robe—the best one—and put it on him; put a ring on his finger and sandals on his feet. And get the fatted calf and kill it, and let us eat and celebrate; for this son of mine was dead and is alive again; he was lost and is found!' And they began to celebrate.

"Now his elder son was in the field; and when he came and approached the house, he heard music and dancing. He called one of the slaves and asked what was going on. He replied, 'Your brother has come, and your father has killed the fatted calf, because he has got him back safe and sound.' Then he became angry and refused to go in. His father came out and began to plead with him. But he answered his father, 'Listen! For all these years I have been working like a slave for you, and I have never disobeyed your command; yet you have never given me even a young goat so that I might celebrate with my friends. But when this son of yours came back, who has devoured your property with prostitutes, you killed the fatted calf for him!' Then the father said to him, 'Son, you are always with me, and all that is mine is yours. But we had to celebrate and rejoice, because this brother of yours was dead and has come to life; he was lost and has been found.'"

Prior to this service a brief account of the achievements and contribution of retiring individuals (from any long service or employment, paid or unpaid) could be published in the church bulletin or magazine.

Prayer for Elders

VOICE 4:
We celebrate and give thanks
For the achievements of those
Who have contributed so much
Over many years,
Whose enduring hope and regard for others
Has made our community
A better place for all.

We remember especially the retiring
And all those leaving long service
Of the church and wider community,
Not so much to mark an ending
But to mark the beginning of a season in life
That may prove to be the most valuable
Both for themselves and for the rest of us,
A time distinguished with the wisdom of years
And with the knowledge and inner strength
So vital for the health and holiness
Of our society and church.

> Bible texts for use in the Meditations on Scripture include Romans 12:9–21 (Marks of the true Christian), Acts 4:32–37 (The believers share their possessions), John 13:1–20 (Jesus washes the disciples' feet), John 10:11–18 (Jesus the good shepherd), Luke 14:7–14 (Humility and hospitality) or a combination of verses or shorter passages like John 13:34–35 (A new commandment), and Matthew 5:13-16 (Salt and light).

You may not feel this great potential
But it is there within you,
And as you allow it opportunity,
Channeling it afresh into our churches,
Our families, and our communities,
We will learn to appreciate you as we should
And find in you a rich source of blessing,
And you may find you have time to accomplish
So much more than you expect:
Time to mentor a young disciple,
Time to pass on your knowledge,
Time to impart your love, strength, and wisdom
To your children or grandchildren
And to all those you meet along the way,
Time perhaps to travel, to widen your perspectives,
And to share your experiences abroad,
Time for greater quietness and the enjoyment of God.

Though our bodies grow old
And our health begins to fail us
Our spirits are renewed daily
And we draw closer to the heart of God
Than ever before,
Reaching into the infinite joys
And all-surpassing peace
That can be found there in abundance.

VOICE 4:
So we pray for all our elders:

May you have a long and pleasant journey,
May you know every hope and happiness,
May you be always honored and cherished in our midst.

A Prayer for the Young

VOICE 5:
God of boisterous spirit and unflinching hope,
We pray now for our children and youth,
For their nurture and protection,
Courage and resilience,
Comfort and assurance.
We pray for their characters,
For honesty and kindness,
For diligence and learning,
For enterprise and optimism,
And we pray for their future
That they might enjoy the untainted beauty
Of a world now so endangered,
Of unspoiled landscapes and pristine seas,
Of clear blue skies and magnificent beasts,
The greatest vistas and the smallest marvels
That they might learn to steward well
All the earth and beyond.

A Prayer of Commissioning

VOICE 6:
God of transformation,
We remember in prayer
And give voice to our support
For all those making a commitment
To work in a new place or role,
Including. . . .

Be with them, God of opportunities,

As they take their first steps.
Give them assurance in the path they have chosen
And the resourcefulness and initiative,
Patience and endurance,
Energy and concentration
That they will need to succeed in their tasks.
May they ask for your guidance in the days ahead,
Coming to decisions in the clarity of love,
For you are with them by day and night,
Their protector and defender,
Bringing blessings out of every choice
Made in sincerity and kindness,
Even those we might at times regret,
For such is the goodness of God.

Communion

VOICE 1:
We come now to the family table of our church,
To the very place where friendships are nourished
And the place for remembering Christ as a host
Who treated his disciples not merely as students
But as sisters and brothers and friends.

VOICE 2:
We leave aside all grief and sorrow
For the comfort of sustaining food and drink
And the companionship of family and friends
Around the table of equity and belonging,
Where we may be ground in the mill
Of company and conversation,
Refreshing and refining our perspectives on life
And returning our attention to the things that matter most,
For our meals break the monotony of the working day
And are the pleasure and delight of the week's end.

Teach us to be generous hosts,
The good in others to see, to toast,
Open hearth and open hand,
These the strength so all can stand.

VOICE 1:
On the eve of his crucifixion, in an upper room
As Jesus shared a final meal with his friends,
He began a ritual that would keep alive
The memory of his sacrifice
And convey a message of forgiveness
Throughout the generations,
For past wrongs and those still to come.
It would satisfy our hunger for God's renewed love,
In times when from love we have strayed.

Jesus took a loaf of bread and blessed it, then he broke it and gave it to his disciples saying, "Take and eat; this is my body. Do this in remembrance of me."

Then he took the cup and gave thanks. Giving it to his disciples he said, "This is my blood of the new covenant, poured out for many for the forgiveness of sins. Do this in remembrance of me."

The bread is passed around the congregation with the words:

The body of Christ, a lattice of friendship.

The wine is passed around the congregation with the words:

The blood of Christ, a covenant of love.

Period of silence

VOICE 2:
The Jews had long made their Passover sacrifices
And their offerings of meat and grain
To be spared from the anger of their God toward sin,
Sin that they had come to believe
Was the cause of their many misfortunes.
But Jesus began a new practice and meal
That would once and for all
Liberate the people from their guilt
And affirm them in the love of God,
A God not of wrath but compassion.
He took wine to symbolize his blood

Flowing to protect his followers
From the cruelty of their oppressors,
For he became their ultimate sacrifice
To bring an end to their offerings of blood.
He took bread to symbolize his body broken,
Lighting a new way to salvation
Through the sacrifice of self
And the forgiveness of others,
A way that could lead to the freeing
Of the captives and slaves,
Yet without hatred and the sword,
Those things that lead only to reprisals
And never-ending conflict.
His was a way that could save the people from tyranny,
From the social, political, and religious elites
And their harassment and repression of the poor,
A way to end the suffering they had known for so long.
It is a long and arduous journey, this way of Christ
With many pioneers still paying the ultimate price,
But it was and is the only way that brings real hope
For lasting peace and prosperity,
Not just for the few but for the many,
For all the inhabitants of the earth.

VOICE 1:
 In the act of communion
Christ revealed divine goodness
As a final triumph over selfishness
Of which his humanity was capable
In the power of the Holy Spirit,
Because he was prepared to die for his friends
In order to unleash a message
Of victory over evil, death, and suffering
And proclaim a better future for the world.
He demonstrated God's willingness to forgive,
For he had already forgiven his betrayer

And those who would renounce him,
Even those who would put him to death.
He renewed for the comfort of the Jews
The covenant of mercy,
A promise made to their ancestors
That they would never be abandoned by their God,
And Jesus crowned that promise
With a new commandment
That they must love one another
As God loves them.

VOICE 2:
Finishing the meal with a hymn
The company went out
And ascended the Mount of Olives.
Reaching the garden of Gethsemane,
Jesus would prepare for his death
In the company of God.

We look back over thousands of years
Admiring nonetheless the stoicism of Christ
In the face of his agony and death
And continue to tell his story to our children
So generations to come will hear of it,
And aspire to his greatness of character,
Knowing the love of God and love for God
That was always his pillar and strength.

Final Prayer and Blessing

VOICE 1:
As our worship draws to its end,
We ask once more for our communities,
In these fast-changing and unpredictable times,
That they might experience a deepening anchor
Of mutual respect and trust,
Of companionship and hope.
Help us to rally around our shared purpose

Our mission of friendship
And the building of a society
In which the realm of God
Is made visible,
One in which all are known
And all are loved.

Amen.

Sung Refrain

EIGHT

Love and Marriage

The liturgy that follows is perfect for a wedding or a renewal of wedding vows. Orders of service should be printed out in booklet form with a card cover saying "Order of Service" and naming below the persons to be wed, the venue, and the date. The order of service should include at least the Marriage Ceremony and the elements of the liturgy where the congregation responds, indicating when they should do so. There should also be a note of who is conducting the service at the start and a note of thanks to those who took part at the end. If there is an appointed or professional photographer, I recommend that there be a request at the beginning of the order of service stating that only he or she should take photographs during the service, in order to limit disruption, as there will be an opportunity for everyone to take photographs during the signing of the register.

If you have relatives or friends who can play musical instruments or sing to a good enough standard, I recommend that you ask them to provide the music for the introit, signing of the register, exit, and the accompaniment for any hymns. This gives a special personal touch to the service and will also save you the cost of hiring professional musicians. It may mean that the music is more distinctive because it will come from whatever the repertoire and whatever the instrument or voice your relatives or friends happen to have available. I recommend they perform something they know and play well, and which conveys the right mood and message but is not necessarily typical wedding music. The planning and rehearsal process is very rewarding and involves more people in the wedding.

If you hire professional musicians for most of the service, it is good at least to have friends or relatives play or sing for five or ten minutes while the register is being signed and photographs are taken. At the end of the liturgy, I have also included the idea of a ten- to fifteen-minute music recital. I can recommend the participation of the bride and groom in the music at this point if either are musicians or singers, but only if the extra nerves this might induce will not impede their enjoyment of the day. At my own wedding I sang a short recital of three classical songs, with my sister accompanying me on the harp and piano, and two friends on the flute and cello. The point in the liturgy where three songs or hymns are played consecutively is an opportunity for an uninterrupted period of contemplative worship. The songs can merge with one another, if the pianist is able to play a bridging melody in which the concluding bars of one piece lead straight into the introductory bars of the next. This helps to maintain a reflective atmosphere that single hymns at different points in a liturgy might easily have broken.

Whether one is religious or entirely secular, a wedding day is one of the most important and special days of a person's life. It is a testament to all that two people can mean to one another, to all they are and have the potential to be together, and all that they hope for. If a person is a member of a community of faith, their wedding day has particular spiritual significance, as it is the outward expression of an inner promise, not only to each other but to God and the wider community to keep vows they have agreed upon.

It is a promise to all those who have invested their trust in the union or who are or will be affected by its success or failure (far more people than modern couples might first assume), to put in their greatest possible effort to make sure the marriage is a success. It is also an act of trust in a divine love that can flow in an ever-deepening channel between two people, throughout the best and worst and most ordinary of times.

If you are preparing to be married and feeling nervous about the future because you have experienced or witnessed the breakdown of relationships and the pain that brings to everyone affected, please take courage in the fact that despite the gloomy statistics we are always hearing, there are many who have walked this way before you and been happily married all their adult lives. There is no reason why you and your partner should not do exactly the same. If you are both loyal and honest, respect one another as equals, are quick to forgive each other, undogmatic in your views and maintain a sense of humor and fun, you are well placed to enjoy a wonderful life together. After your wedding it is good to remind yourselves regularly of why you got married, what you love about each other, and of the vows and promises you made, so you can keep putting them into practice.

I would really encourage brides and bridegrooms to write their own prayer or poem to be read during the service or during the reception either by themselves or by a friend. Just as with the music, this is a great opportunity to introduce a personal element to the day. It encourages the creative involvement of the couple in proceedings, and a poem is something that can be kept forever as a keepsake and perhaps even framed. Below is the poem I wrote and read at my own wedding reception as an example of a personal contribution. It was inspired by that profound sense of place that we humans enjoy, and in this instance, the context of the British Isles and Edinburgh, Scotland, in which our love was born and grew.

Sacred Moments

Here in this city of arresting views
And the thinnest and purest of light,
Where hearts are broken and made whole again
Under ephemeral skies and racing cloud,
What can we speak of but friendship?
Adrift as we are in the vastness of space and time,
On a lonely pilgrimage around the dying star
From which we came,
It is friendship that ties one to another,
That braves the perils of the journey.
I cannot help but love these temperate isles
Of roses, thistles, daffodils, and shamrock.
Small places of questioning and quaint delights,
Of the heroic story, the subtle gesture and the distant memory,
Places whose conviviality and open fires
Have dwindled under the weight of riches
But are longed for with increasing intensity,

A renewal of the kindness we have suppressed
And the fairness that won for our little corner
The respect of the nations.
I cannot help but love still more this fragile globe that carries us,
Its colorful peoples and creatures, from the elegant to the eccentric,
Where private exchanges and the sayings of the few are precious,
But still we are one in our humanity
And our language universal,
Sounds and signals that must be those of love,
Of acceptance, of compassion, of hope.

Going then soon, from this our city of turret and crag,
Of steep climbs and horizontal rain
Where the echoes of the ages are preserved
In gray granite and sandstone
And the summer skies refuse to darken,
We will leave one love to nurture another,
Forever the impression on our souls
Of Scotland's hills and secret glens,
Her islands of the clearest waters and the whitest of sands,
A wild landscape where angels lie yet undisturbed,
Where the descent of heaven already meets the earth.

Though buffeted by whirling gales and draped in snow,
Unguarded smiles were exchanged here
In a quiet place, where love was enough.
I am grateful for the little path we tread together,
My dearest friend and I,
Through this swirling sphere of blue,
Carrying one another's load along the way.
I thank him for his constant love,
For the moments and years we have already shared.
But there are no words for these, only silence,
For even poetry will fail to capture them.
So we speak again of friendship,
And we hope to travel alongside each of you
To meet in new and stirring times

As pilgrims of one consciousness, following one light
In sacramental moments such as these.

The *Liturgy of Love* helps us to move away from the traditional and rather impersonal ceremony where most of the guests are not engaged with the words and are preoccupied instead with thoughts about the dress or the promise of a wedding banquet. It endeavors to bring the meaning of marriage and the sacramental or transforming presence of God to the center of the proceedings, making the service one the couple and guests will remember for the rest of their lives. It should inspire a collective spiritual experience, in which everyone present is touched by the love of God as it is celebrated and moved by the power of marriage to enhance and enrich the love between all human beings in society.

The liturgy is suitable for either a small reflective service with guests gathered in an informal and intimate semicircular arrangement, either standing or sitting, or for a larger, more formal setting. If neither bride nor groom feels able to take part by writing or reading a prayer or poem, a friend or relative may well be equipped to do the honors instead. The months of wedding planning are extremely busy ones, but it is well worth putting in a little extra effort to add that personal touch to the service, which, after all, is the focal point and purpose of the day. The sacramental act of marriage takes place during the service and centers, of course, on the Marriage Ceremony and vows.

All too many couples end up glossing over its preparation and most of its content, even on the day, leaving it to a minister or other local official, while they focus most attention on planning the evening celebrations. The party afterward may well be unforgettable, but while there will be plenty of parties to come, there will hopefully be no further occasions to have one's own wedding service!

The preparation for a powerful and poignant service requires the couple to completely open up to each other in the months beforehand, and perhaps also to discuss their relationship with an external party such as their local minister in addition to trusted friends and family in preparation for married life. They should give voice to their deepest hopes and fears and to the nature of their faith as it relates to their relationship. They should each feel comfortable to be open about their vulnerabilities and able to communicate their particular needs. This manner of preparation encourages the couple to work on establishing the very best of foundations for their life together, foundations of openness, honesty, equality, and respect. A preparation period allows for greater assurance and confidence that the step they are taking is right for both people, and teases out any problems that need to be resolved prior to marriage. It may in a few cases help individuals to realize and admit that there are serious problems, such as an unequal balance of respect or power in the relationship, and prevent an unwise marriage from going ahead.

It is also important to note that practical subjects that can cause a great deal of disagreement, such as finances, children, careers, and where to live should be discussed in detail before marriage takes place, however boring and unromantic this may seem. Both people should be frank both about what they are bringing to the marriage in material terms and what existing plans they have for the future.

Marriage is the most wonderful journey two people can make together. Though there will always be arguments, and two imperfect human beings living in close quarters will always hurt and disappoint one another at times, the rewards of companionship and mutual support far outweigh the small sacrifices of our pride, privacy, and self-centeredness that such an intimate relationship demands. Marriage is also still upheld, by those who report on social statistics, even in the most secular of circles, as the most successful institution for providing a secure and stable environment in which children can thrive and achieve their potential.

It is also, therefore, the best foundation for a healthy society. Marriage teaches the art of shared life and love to the next generation and gives space for the fullest expression of unfettered affection and the most unconditional of human loves, that between husband and wife and between parents and children. Importantly, successful marriages have great potential to maintain harmony and understanding between the sexes. When based on good principles of fairness and equality, marriages lead to greater mutual respect between the sexes in society at large.

For this reason, marriage between a man and a woman has a distinct significance and purpose within wider society. It helps to ensure that women have the protection they need as the physically smaller, and therefore more easily exploited sex, especially during times of particular vulnerability such as pregnancy and childbearing, from the tendency of the bigger more muscular half of the species to take advantage and demote or intimidate them into submission. The *Liturgy of Love* is written to encourage this essential role of marriage, though with a few small changes in wording it could be easily adapted for a marriage taking place between persons of the same gender.

Even the apostle Paul, in a time of great inequality between genders and between ethnic and social groups, recognized that equality and oneness should be the ultimate goal of faith:

> There is no longer Jew or Greek, there is no longer slave or free, there is no longer male and female; for all of you are one in Christ Jesus. (Gal. 3:28)

Through mixed-race marriages and marriages across social and economic divides, increasing numbers of people learn to appreciate difference, overcome prejudices, and live peaceably with one another. Family relationships bring about the deepest loyalties among us, beyond that of most friendships, and so it is especially by intermarriage that more permanent bridges can be built between divided communities. With regard to same sex-marriages, the most common argument against them seems to come from a deep-seated fear that they will somehow undermine marriages between heterosexuals and "the family."

I, however, have not seen any evidence suggesting that what would always be a small number of same-sex marriages would have any deleterious effects on the vast majority of opposite-sex marriages and their advantages for women. Same-sex marriages, being between people who are more matched in their physical strength, career opportunities, pay, and so on, are indeed a better model of equality than many opposite-sex marriages, where there are sadly still significant imbalances of power even in the most liberal of societies. Marriage being so important for equality and so beneficial for men and women alike (married men have better health and live longer!), it is vital that our societies encourage and reward it, and that we respectfully point out to younger generations the disadvantages of cohabiting for long periods, for their emotional, physical and mental health and happiness, not forgetting also to explain the legal and financial benefits that often apply to marriage.

I have known many women who have felt they have had to live with a man for many years and have children with him prior to marriage because there are so few men willing to make such a commitment that it would always have come to a choice between accepting a less-than-satisfactory arrangement with someone they love or the loneliness of singleness. Clearly there are a lot of men out there who are rather cowardly and are reluctant to commit, even though it would be far more likely to benefit both parties than have any adverse effects on the relationship or their individual freedoms.

Marriage arrived at with the right attitudes and intentions is in fact a liberating and empowering experience for both partners, rather than something that restricts and imprisons, the latter being the suggestion of many an unfortunate joke. People who are really well suited feel that together they can better express themselves and achieve their potential, even if each has to modify their plans made originally as single people to accommodate one another. Compromises, one must remember, have to be reached in any relationship whether sealed by marriage or not. Marriage brings freedoms in new and unexpected ways as each person grows in character and confidence because of the love, support, and wisdom of the other. There needs to be more open celebration of good marriages and their many joys to counter the jokes and the negative press, combined with a degree of moral and social pressure toward this kind of marriage and a lot more encouragement from happily married friends and family in order to help to give young people the best possible chance at building a successful family life.

A common excuse given these days by the noncommitted is a lack of wedding funds, exacerbated by the extreme commercialization of weddings that gives the impression we all have enormous and unrealistic expectations. However, this really does not hold water, since most people know that the best weddings are certainly not always the expensive ones. With a little imagination, a budget wedding need not look cheap, and may indeed be a much more memorable and meaningful occasion for its simplicity and personal touches. The wedding liturgy below encourages an attention to details which do not cost anything but which are the most important aspects of any wedding event.

THE LITURGY OF LOVE: FOR A WEDDING

The congregation stands for the entrance or procession of the bride

Sung Refrain (*entrance music*)

Minister or Service Leader:

Welcome

We have gathered here in celebration
To share in the joy of *Name* and *Name*
And surround them with our love
As they set out to become one
In the adventure of marriage,
We will witness their vows,
Not only as a legal formality
Or social rite of passage
But as a sacrament
That changes us within,
Tapping our deepest dimensions,
Reaching into the love of God
And plumbing its depth of riches,
Those that give us meaning,
Our value and our purpose.
And as it was for the first couples
Among the disciples of Christ,

So it will be for *Name* and *Name,*
Who will come to know
Beyond every doubt,
Confirmed in the mystery of marriage,
That God is love,
And those who dwell in love
Dwell in God and God in them.
It is this love we celebrate
And to which we pledge support,
Asking God's blessing on *Name* and *Name*
As they commit to one another
Before God and before us.

Congregation sits

Reading by a relative or friend of the couple:

Poem:
The Lovers' Nook

In a lovers' nook among the trees, where hazy summers passed,
They gazed at the sky and pheasants courting, over the fields of grass,
Then the quiet fall was as sweet as spring, for all was understood.
And in colored leaves they made their nest, right there at the neck of
     the wood.

The winter frost brought a bitter cold, but there by earth and flame,
Each within the other's arms did flourish all the same.
The vows that staid them in the gale, white roses in her hair,
Would never be forgotten by the love resounding there.

With every year and every tide, new troubles came to roost,
But each full with the other's strength, all sorrows quickly loosed,
For nothing could disturb them long, love's comforts always near
And love's forgiveness quick to come for each repentant tear.

He took her to the meadow; she took him to the brook.
They skated on a frozen lake, exchanged a gleeful look,

And setting sail for distant shores, the sea spray in their faces,
Their lives one story now to tell, of love and all its places.

Love took them to a higher plane, a flight above the skies,
Where God, no more a stranger, was reflected in their eyes,
And walking through life's garden, its fruit in bright array,
Moments of eternity, were etched upon their way.

Sung Refrain

THE MARRIAGE CEREMONY

The congregation sits.

Minister or Service Leader:

Name and *Name*,
As you begin a shared future,
Trusting in the love each has for the other,
You will become a sign
That defines a life of love,
Not only for one another,
But for all who know and hear of you.
With your promises,
The mystery and grace of God
Find a home and are made known,
Renewing and enhancing life
As the love between you deepens.
Exceeding all of human expectation,
You will experience the power of divine love
As you help keep each other on course
Through times of uncertainty
And share one another's desires,
Longings, dreams, and memories,
And all that touches the inmost parts
Of our hearts and minds.
Called to live faithfully together
To mutual love and respect,
Called to support one another

With tenderness
And to enjoy one another with delight,
You are encouraged to risk more
And so to gain more.
The companionship and comfort of this union
Is the fullest form of self-giving
And mutual commitment
Of body, mind, emotion, and spirit,
And upon the foundation of marriage
Family life may continue
For the well-being and stability of all,
A society where human dignity and happiness
May flourish and abound.
So, *Name* and *Name,* on this your special day
You seek to be joined together
In confidence that this step
Affirming your relationship
Will lead to the strengthening and deepening
Of lifelong companionship
And enrichment and joy in your lives.

Prayer of Occasion

God of our past, present, and future,
We thank you for your goodness
And for the gift of love,
For the richness and variety of life,
For the joy and fulfillment of deep relationships.
We thank you for *Name* and *Name*
As they stand before us and before you now,
For all the experience of life
That has brought them to this moment,
For the joy and hope that comes from sharing
Both strength and vulnerability,
Times of difficulty and challenge
As well as periods of ease and prosperity.
We thank you for the happiness and goodness

They have known and shared with each other already,
For all their families mean to them,
For all they mean to their families,
For the love and affection with which they are surrounded
And still upheld by all those close to them.
We thank you for the joy *Name* and *Name*
Have found in one another,
For friendship as it has deepened into love,
A love which found its way to certainty and trust
As they commit themselves to one another now.
We pray that their relationship will continue to be blessed
And enhanced through the working of your grace
And the support of family and friends.
Give them the strength, the resilience,
The fondness and affection
That will enable them to keep
The promises they are about to make
In the sight of God and in the light of Christ.

Amen.

The vows, exchange of rings, and declaration

The minister says to the couple:
Name and *Name*, as a seal to the vows you are about to make,
will you give each other your right hand?

He says
Before God and in the presence of our families and friends, I promise to love you, comfort you, honor you, and protect you, as long as we both shall live.

She says
Before God and in the presence of our families and friends, I promise to love you, comfort you, honor you, and protect you, as long as we both shall live.

The minister says to the couple:

As a symbol of all that you have promised and all that you will share, these rings are given and received. They are the signs of your commitment to one another—that you take each other, to have and to hold from this day forward, for better or worse, for richer for poorer, in sickness and in health, to love and to cherish, till death do you part.

The minister says to the congregation:
Will you, the families and friends of *Name* and *Name*, support and uphold them in their marriage, now and in the years to come?

Congregation answers:

We will.

The minister says to the couple:
Name and *Name*, since you have now pledged yourselves to one another in the covenant of marriage and have affirmed your love for one another, I declare you to be husband and wife.

The couple kneel

The minister says to the couple:
The God of heaven keep you
And be gracious unto you;
The light of Christ
Shine within you
And give you peace.

*The bride and groom rise, embrace, and exchange a kiss;
the congregation stands and applauds.*

We proclaim the promise of God's love:

**Love unending,
Love divine,
Ever yours and ever mine.**

Three Reflective Songs (chosen by the couple)

Bride and Bridegroom's Poem:

The congregation sits.

An Exchange of Hearts

Bride:

The fields of love do not wilt away
Nor do they lose their bloom,
For love's treasures, like wild flowers
Are found the year through.
She sometimes rests beneath us
And cradles our sleeping heads.
She sometimes grasps, our hearts arresting,
Bringing tears of happiness.

It is in this way that I love you
And pray to love you always,
With courage and without regret,
Through seasons colored and gray,
Trusting you with my tender heart
That you will guard it always,
And taking yours in my own hands
With joy and with gladness,
Knowing no greater honor
Than to keep it as my own.

Bridegroom's Response:

The springs of love do not run dry
Nor are her seas contained,
For true love spreads her wings forever
In a tide unchanging.
She gives away her boundless joys
In matchless generosity.
So we may share them with abandon
And cherish them within.

It is in this way that I love you
And pray to love you always
Unguarded and without reserve
Trusting you with my fragile heart
That you will hold it gently

And taking yours for my own
With awe and wonder
Knowing no greater privilege
Than to keep it safe and warm.

Meditation on Scripture

Reading by a friend or relative of the couple:

1 Corinthians 13

If I speak in the tongues of mortals and of angels, but do not have love, I am a noisy gong or a clanging cymbal. And if I have prophetic powers, and understand all mysteries and all knowledge, and if I have all faith, so as to remove mountains, but do not have love, I am nothing. If I give away all my possessions, and if I hand over my body so that I may boast, but do not have love, I gain nothing.

Love is patient; love is kind; love is not envious or boastful or arrogant or rude. It does not insist on its own way; it is not irritable or resentful; it does not rejoice in wrongdoing, but rejoices in the truth. It bears all things, believes all things, hopes all things, endures all things.

Love never ends. But as for prophecies, they will come to an end; as for tongues, they will cease; as for knowledge, it will come to an end. For we know only in part, and we prophesy only in part; but when the complete comes, the partial will come to an end. When I was a child, I spoke like a child, I thought like a child, I reasoned like a child; when I became an adult, I put an end to childish ways. For now we see in a mirror, dimly, but then we will see face to face. Now I know only in part; then I will know fully, even as I have been fully known. And now faith, hope, and love abide, these three; and the greatest of these is love.

Prayer of Thanksgiving

Minister or Service Leader:

Eternal God,
We thank you for the many ways
Love enters our lives
And for the opportunities for joy

Bible texts for use in the Meditations on Scripture include Mark 10:2–9 (Becoming one flesh), Romans 12:1–2, 9–21 (Marks of the true Christian), Psalm 84, Philippians 4:4–9, and Colossians 3:12–16.

And fulfillment marriage brings.
We thank you for all that this day means to *Name* and *Name*.
And to their families and friends,
The culmination of careful planning and preparation
And the start of a new stage in their journey together.
We ask your blessing over the years ahead
When times are good
But especially when they are hard,
May they live in harmony and true companionship
Throughout their life together,
Seeking one another's welfare,
Bearing one another's burdens,
And sharing one another's joys.
Go before them in the days to come
That they may know the truth,
The peace, and the love that comes from you alone.
May they be strengthened and guided
In the way of generosity and compassion
And neighborly concern,
And may there be a welcome
For both friends and strangers in their home.
At this time of happiness and celebration,
Help each one of us to live
With compassion and integrity,
To remember those in need
And to give thanks for those dear ones
Who have influenced our lives for good
And, having walked this way before us,
Are now safe with you forever.

All: Amen.

Final Blessing
Every blessing be yours,
Name and *Name,*
Who made in God's image
Today become a sign
Of God's faithful love for us,
The greatest of loves.

May this love of God,
The grace of Christ,
And the presence of the Holy Spirit
Be with us all
Forevermore.

All: **Amen.**

Signing of the Register (If this is your church tradition)

Opportunity to take photographs

Music Recital

Opportunity to take photographs

Exit of the Bridal Party

Note of thanks to the minister and those taking part as musicians and readers

NINE

Death and Funerals

The Celtic-style *Funeral Liturgy* is a service of solidarity with both the grieving and the dead. It is suitable for the funeral of either an adult or child. Its perspective is that death is a part of a wider circle of life, rather than an ending, and marks the transition to a new stage in a person's eternal existence in God. Like the other liturgies, it challenges the taboo surrounding death that is prevalent in Western society. The service encourages a fuller participation of relatives and friends of the deceased in the leadership of the service and in the deliverance of verse and eulogy.

Much of religion in its widest sense has been constructed around death. Fundamental to all religions, for example, are the ways of dealing with the practicalities of death, such as the treatment of the corpse, and ways of coping with grief, honoring and remembering the dead, and facing our own death. This liturgy hopes to go further toward meeting our spiritual needs with respect to death in the twenty-first century, which have in fact changed little since the first.

The liturgy is inspired by the "Celtic" Christian traditions of Scotland, Ireland, and Wales, which, though largely modern in construction, despite some of their claims to ancient origins, are nonetheless movements that have greatly enhanced the beauty, gentleness, and subtlety of Christian worship for many people around the globe in recent times. Its particular features are the comforting emphasis on nature and the imitation of its perpetual rhythms, and its affirmation of the mysterious, with imaginative visions of a spirit world alongside ours, perhaps existing in parallel dimensions, and sometimes marvelously overlapping.

It is, therefore, the ideal form in which to compose a liturgy on a subject as sensitive and enigmatic as death. The Celtic style is an

unashamed celebration of romance and nostalgia concerning what
has passed, and of the imagination and the natural world in the present, the very things many of us instinctually turn to for comfort when
someone dies.

THE LITURGY OF FAREWELLS:
FOR A FUNERAL

*Relatives and friends gather in silence to lay wreaths and flowers
and to quietly greet one another.*

*Relatives and friends take their places around the burial site
or take their seats in the church or crematorium.*

Welcome and Prayer

VOICE 1:
Comfort, comfort, O my soul,
In loss be near us present,
God unchanging, God of love.
Send forth your dove of peace
And your strength in arms
As we commit our soul-friend
To the Healer's keeping,
To the house of God.

Sung Refrain

VOICE 2:

Poem:
A Celtic Twilight

White sands, where rest the lapping waves
Stretch out to deepest blue, and golden rays,
O watery home for distant falling suns
Whose smoldering blood-red color runs.

**Across to the isle of angels, you are gone
By lamp and oar of Christ and pilgrim song.**

An eagle's cry resounding in the air,
The soaring herald of your arrival there,
And banks of grasses pointing in the wind
Turn the heads of creatures furred and finned.

Across to the isle of angels, you are gone
By lamp and oar of Christ and pilgrim song.

I watch from distant shores of earthly kind
And hope for remnant of you there to find
The echoes of your voice within the wood
The peace of death a solace understood.

Across to the isle of angels, you are gone
By lamp and oar of Christ and pilgrim song.

Our headland meets a cloud that's bowed with rain,
Who asks to wash away her sorrow's grain
Then thunders from the yawning skies a flood,
The cattle standing stalwart in the mud.

Across to the isle of angels, you are gone
By lamp and oar of Christ and pilgrim song.

Tell us of that place, O silent star,
Where clear stillness breaks the rolling harr,
For the fireside of the Healer flickers bright:
A journey's end for travelers of the night.

Across to the isle of angels, you are gone
By lamp and oar of Christ and pilgrim song.

In green of leaf and stem life seems for keeping,
But to God alone is known the times for weeping.
And now we live to honor what was lost,
The boatman having waived the pilgrim's cost.

Across to the isle of angels, you are gone
By lamp and oar of Christ and pilgrim song.

The angels line the pier, where moored at last
Their piercing eyes upon your spirit cast,

And there in presence of the heavenly host
You look no more to our ethereal coast.

Across to the isle of angels, you are gone
By lamp and oar of Christ and pilgrim song.

So take the warmth of our shared moments with you.
Take the laughter, take the smiles there, too,
And pray for us left in the veil by name,
Our stories known but tell them all the same.

Across to the isle of angels, you are gone
By lamp and oar of Christ and pilgrim song.

Invitation

You are invited to partake in a period of personal reflection
and the lighting of candles as a symbol of prayer for the deceased.

Music can be played or sung by a friend or relative during this time.

VOICE 1:
We look to the hills
For the coming of salvation,
To God our defender and our help.

May your good and holy will
Sustain us day by day,
Forgiving us our sins
And delivering us from evil,
For yours is the earth and sky,
The seas and all the heavens,
And yours the power and glory,
Now and forevermore.

The Reading of Eulogies

The eulogies may end with personal prayers
for the deceased or a poem or passage from wider literature.

Burial or Cremation

VOICE 1:
We join together in prayer for [*Name*]
As she/he passes through death into new life,
Safe in a love that bridges every rushing stream.
And as Jesus died, was buried, and then rose again,
We take courage and pray with resurrection hope
For his/her eternal dwelling in the heavenly city of God.

As the coffin is lowered into the ground
or withdrawn into the furnace:

[*Full name*]
In a world of spirit,
At the heart of God,
Hear still a mortal's blessing:

May the sun shine warmly at your back
And the grass beneath your feet be soft.
May a gentle breeze refresh your face
And the dove of peace rest upon your shoulder
Until we meet again.

Meditation on Scripture

The Psalms provide excellent material for meditations at funerals, including Psalms 23, 84, 90, and 121.

VOICE 3:

The Inescapable God, Psalm 139:1–18

O Lord, you have searched me and known me.
You know when I sit down and when I rise up;
you discern my thoughts from far away.
You search out my path and my lying down,
and are acquainted with all my ways.

Even before a word is on my tongue,
O Lord, you know it completely.
You hem me in, behind and before,
and lay your hand upon me.
Such knowledge is too wonderful for me;
it is so high that I cannot attain it.

Where can I go from your spirit?
Or where can I flee from your presence?
If I ascend to heaven, you are there;
if I make my bed in Sheol, you are there.
If I take the wings of the morning
and settle at the farthest limits of the sea,
even there your hand shall lead me,
and your right hand shall hold me fast.
If I say, "Surely the darkness shall cover me,
and the light around me become night,"
even the darkness is not dark to you;
the night is as bright as the day,
for darkness is as light to you.

For it was you who formed my inward parts;
you knit me together in my mother's womb.
I praise you, for I am fearfully and wonderfully made.
Wonderful are your works;
that I know very well.
My frame was not hidden from you,
when I was being made in secret,
intricately woven in the depths of the earth.
Your eyes beheld my unformed substance.
In your book were written
all the days that were formed for me,
when none of them as yet existed.
How weighty to me are your thoughts, O God!
How vast is the sum of them!
I try to count them—they are more than the sand;
I come to the end—I am still with you.

Sung Refrain

Final Prayer and Blessing

VOICE 1:
Farewell, farewell departed
From your life in the palm of God's hand
To your death in the same,
You are not forgotten.

In spite of the sorrow of our parting ways
We find warmth in the memory of your days,
Days that are etched in the mind of God,
Beginning in love and ending in the same,
A love existing before all things
And in whom all things are held together,
A love in collision of matter and spirit
Where the living and the dead are one.

VOICE 1:
In body as in soul you are reborn,
For each returns to the sands that gave them birth,
Where atoms rearrange and reconfigure
And in all that springs then from the ground
We are reincarnate,
Earth to flesh, flesh to earth,
In that everlasting circle of life,
Each moment immeasurable,
Fleetingly precious
This unfathomable diversity of form
From the dust of glinting stars.

> Entry and exit music can be played for a funeral indoors. For an outdoor funeral, piping or some other music may be played at the start and finish of the service as guests are coming or going.

TEN

Incarnation

The following Christmas liturgy marks the centrality of the Incarnation for the Christian faith. It signifies in what was a scandalous way for its time, God's identification with human flesh, all its accompanying weaknesses and afflictions and even the full horror of a body brutally maimed and killed. The life of Jesus is perhaps the greatest example of divine revelation as perceived in ordinary human encounters and conversations. His disciples certainly saw in him the manifestations of God.

Jesus represents the personhood of a God who would otherwise be a wholly abstract entity with whom communication might seem difficult or even impossible. Here is a God to whom ordinary laboring people can come in person rather than merely ponder in their minds, one who can be approached with the ordinary language of praise, requests, and outpourings of emotion, as one might approach a friend or relative, and just like King David approached God in his psalms, without having to have one's address filtered through a priestly caste and the rules and rituals of the temple. Jesus took old metaphors for God, such as shepherd, king, father, and master, and combined them in new ways in his stories to create a concept of God that would be much more familiar and accessible to the poorest classes, of which he was a member.

Jesus' life and teachings became in themselves, for many people, divine confirmation that the poor were equal to the rich in the eyes of God and that a new intimacy was possible between God and every human being regardless of social status. Jesus is still, for many, the face of God, or one of several faces of God, even though that face is typically the stylized medieval portrayal of Jesus (a white man with chiseled features, a beard, and a serene expression) or perhaps some other imagined appearance that corresponds conveniently to whatever ideal of beauty one's own culture endorses.

213

In recent times, there have been portraits and sculptures of the face of Jesus based on what is now known about the appearance of the Hebrew people of his day, but though these may come closer, we will never have an exact image. A "perfect" human face, either male or female (such as the female Christs of very early and very modern Christian art), has always been the preferred way to envision God. It is a means, not only of inventing God in our ideal image, but of getting around the difficult problem of worshiping the abstract.

It is not an easy task to rise above the ego and surpass our ordinary emotions to fully appreciate the otherness and the transcendence of God, the God who is more than and better than us and always slightly out of reach. This is why Christianity has always clung to its saints and martyrs, its symbols, icons, relics, and priestly castes. When God seems remote, at least one of these representations is guaranteed to be close at hand and real and tangible to us. For example, saints, our Christian predecessors, whose lives one can sometimes read about, put flesh on the bones of faith when it appears thin and insubstantial, as it does at times for all of us, giving a richness, depth, and consistency to the Christian life.

Celebrations of the birth of Jesus at Christmas and the resurrection of Jesus at Easter also provide stability by creating predictable rhythms, helping to mark the passing of time and giving us anchors and reminders of the most important and distinctive aspects of our faith, the life and teachings of Jesus and the insights into salvation they give us.

As with the *Easter Liturgy* or *Liturgy of Salvation*, the Christmas liturgy can be characterized by a little more theater and pageantry befitting this important period of festivities, as long as it is in good taste, simple, and elegant, and does not disturb the reflective atmosphere. With very low lighting, lit candles (floating candles) can be placed in a large plate or bowl of water. Communion can be carried out using panettone (or fruit bread) and mulled wine in order to create an experience special to the Christmas period that reflects the richness, cheerfulness, and generosity of God. Small changes like this can stimulate new thought and are valuable in refreshing a common aspect of worship that might otherwise become routine.

In the secular mind, Christmas is associated with the appreciation and enjoyment of family, romance, generosity, quaint and eclectic traditions both old and new, hospitality, and fun. All of these are, or should be, important aspects of Christian and church life, and especially our Christmas festivities. Unfortunately, rather than exploiting the great potential of Christmas, by setting an example of friendliness, sharing, and merriment worthy of admiration, many Christians retreat to obscure, tedious, and outdated rituals and spend their energies bemoaning the commercialization of Christmas and the shrine to materialism erected each year by the secular world in its name.

Though Jesus was a simple prophet, teacher, and social reformer and Christ, the fullness of God, a later construction of the early church, Jesus may still be seen as an incarnation of divinity. This does not require that he be either fully divine or the only such incarnation. As mentioned earlier, the nature of Jesus was in contention for several centuries before the political and religious elite chose their favored definition. Other religions, of course, claim their own incarnations and representatives of divinity that they might call avatars or appearances, but the impact of Jesus has been so great and so wide that some of the most ancient faiths, such as Hinduism, have at times even been willing to incorporate him into their pantheon of divine manifestations.

The Christian traditions, especially the Roman Catholic and Orthodox ones, also have their other divine incarnations in Mary the virgin mother of God, the saints, and the angels of the Lord, though they might try to formulate their natures differently from Christ's in terms of formal doctrine. Despite the insistence of the clerical elites that these beings are subordinate to the incarnation of Christ, in many cultures, Mary (or sometimes even a local saint little known outside the area) is so much the embodiment and agent of divinity in the religious practices and prayers of the people that she has superseded Jesus as the more popular image and incarnation of God. Mary's enormous influence no doubt attests to the deep inadequacy of the exclusively male conception of God in Father, Son, and Holy Ghost that male clerics have asserted through the ages.

The *Christmas Liturgy of the Incarnation*, like the other liturgies, seeks to draw upon a more open theology of incarnation while maintaining that Jesus is the cornerstone of the Christian faith. It acknowledges that on account of Jesus' maleness, Hebrewness, and every other limiting aspect of being one human being, he cannot represent divinity in its fullness, but he can be the linchpin upon which hang the great many insights and traditions of one of the most compelling and comprehensive of faiths.

THE CHRISTMAS LITURGY OF THE INCARNATION

A Christmas tree and hanging decorations for people to write their prayers on could be provided. Rolled up miniscrolls, decorated on the outside and with a thread attached, are ideal for this. They can be written on in the inside and rolled up again. They make attractive and easy hangings and maintain privacy regarding the prayers they contain.

Welcoming Poem

Ring the Church Bells

VOICE 1:
Ring the church bells, for Christmas is here!
Come glitter, come tinsel, come snow,
The fir and the spruce and the pine evergreen
While the fairy lights twinkle and glow.

Ring the church bells, for Christmas is here!
With scent of mulled wine and mince pies,
Vanilla pods, citrus, and cinnamon sticks,
And flames that reflect in our eyes.

Ring the church bells, for Christmas is here!
With crimson and silver and gold,
Visions of reindeer and Santa Claus
And the magical stories of old.

Ring the church bells, for Christmas is here!

With berries and fruited loaves,
With holly and ivy and mistletoe
And gingerbread, crackers, and cloves.

Ring the church bells, for Christmas is here!
Come frankincense, symbol of birth.
See the robin alight on the garden gate,
Hear the sounds of carols and mirth.

Ring the church bells, for Christmas is here!
With stuffing and turkey roast,
Our gifts placed lovingly under the tree
While we raise a cheerful toast.

Ring the church bells, for Christmas is here!
Let everyone gather within,
For the soaring tones of choristers
Have the joys of heaven to sing.

> A pleasant-sounding bell can be rung by the reader as he or she reads the first line of each verse.

Invitation

While the music is playing (or choristers are singing), you are invited to light a floating candle representing yourself or your family as a symbol of your presence and belonging with God and all those who follow Christ. Launch it gently onto the water and watch as it joins the others.

> A large bowl or saucer of water on the central table can be used for this. Several smaller bowls can be used if your church or other venue does not have a suitably large or aesthetically pleasing bowl. If your church has a large font or baptismal pool, this could be used and the service could take place with everyone gathered around it.

VOICE 2:
My mouth proclaims the glory of God
Whose works unravel the mysteries of the age.
In his power and in her strength enduring
Was life on earth created and sustained,
The sun by day, the moon by night to guide us,
A tiny child, once sent to light the way.

VOICE 3:
A voice cries out in the wilderness:
"Prepare the way! Make straight the paths of the Lord!"
For you are called to discipleship
To the one who teaches God's wisdom
And shows us God's love.

We listen to the voice
Crying out in the desert
And clear the tangled paths
To our minds and hearts
So God can enter and take root.
We endeavor to turn the ears of all
To the voice of the Author of Life,
Making straight her paths
Throughout our homes and cities,
Our schools and colleges,
The places of both work and leisure.
We invite the God of love
Into every human exchange
Of word, of glance and touch,
Of money, material, and time.
For we desire to honor God afresh,
Studying the teachings of Jesus,
Who came into the world
Longing to heal and free us
From suffering and sin
And to share with both high and lowly born
The most excellent way of all,

A way in which courage and humility
Are united in love.
For we hear and take to heart
The teachings of Christ
Growing in character and maturity
As we meditate on the wisdom of God
And delight in the moral law that keeps us safe.

Sung Refrain

Still-Speaking Parable:
The Life of Jesus

VOICE 2:

Jesus, the son of a carpenter, was born in Galilee, a troubled province of the Roman Empire. Here, the Jewish people followed their Hebrew religious traditions and revered the instructions given through the law and the prophets. Jesus received a divine calling to invite his fellow Jews to penitence and inner reform with a view to the imminent rule of God. His message went beyond the preaching of Jonah or the Wisdom of Solomon and he appeared to fulfill the prophets' expectations of the Messiah (the anointed one) who the Jews believed would come to save God's people.

VOICE 3:

A community of disciples gathered around Jesus and he commissioned an inner circle of apostles (or missionaries) to proclaim the good news (or Gospel) that God's realm was now at hand. This Gospel was not primarily addressed to the rich and powerful but to the poor, those who worked the land and for whom the many rules of the Pharisees (or religious leaders), particularly those concerning ritual purity, were onerous and impractical. Some Pharisees were sympathetic to Jesus' passionate and earnest cause, but others felt threatened by it. Jesus presented many challenges to ordinary morality. He broke the rules of the religious elite, such as the Sabbath laws, which were a burden to the poor and sometimes an obstacle to moral righteousness. He claimed it was the humble and the poor in spirit who would inherit the earth and the realm of God.

VOICE 2:

Jesus told his disciples to love their enemies and to refrain from judging others if they did not wish to be judged themselves. He taught them that they could not serve both God and money and that not only their actions but even their thoughts would be under the scrutiny of God. He taught that if they forgave those who injured them, they too would be forgiven by God. Jesus summarized his own teachings and all the law and the prophets by urging his disciples to love God with all their hearts, souls, minds, and strength and to love their neighbors as themselves, treating others as they themselves would wish to be treated.

VOICE 3:

Jesus believed that the realm of God was so close and the proclamation of the Gospel so urgent that it had priority even over attending a family funeral. The calling to follow Jesus' movement for religious and social revolution was, despite its peaceful nature, extremely costly, with its many difficult moral demands and the risk of persecution. The gate was narrow and the way was hard that led to life. His message, however, captured the hopes and imaginations of a large following, and this alarmed not only Herod, the Roman governor of the province, but also the ruling Jewish classes, especially the Sadducees, a religious and social elite.

VOICE 2:

Jesus foresaw that his mission to preach the Gospel and make disciples would result in divided households, social conflicts, and martyrdom. Roman governors of Judea regarded claimants to be the messiah as inherently seditious, and Pontius Pilate was persuaded that he needed to have Jesus executed to avert serious disorder. They executed Jesus by public crucifixion, a method which prolonged as far as possible the torture and the pain of the preliminary beatings and humiliation, in order to provide an exemplary deterrent.

VOICE 3:

However, Jesus' disciples became convinced that the tomb where his body was laid had been found awe-inspiringly empty and that Jesus' presence was still with them as they studied the Hebrew scriptures and prayed. They could recount a list of those to whom the risen Lord had appeared, and the disciples were ready to sacrifice their lives for the proclamation of the Gospel. Jesus became immortalized, victorious over suffering and even death, and remained in this way with his followers, a comforting presence, a moral compass, a great hope for their own salvation.

Invitation

While the music is playing, you are invited to light another floating candle, this time for those relatives and friends now dead whom you are missing this Christmas. Launch it on the water and watch as the little fleet representing the dead mingles with that which represents the living forming a large cloud of witnesses to the glory of God.

VOICE 2:
The candles represent ourselves
And those gone before us,
A flotilla of pilgrims,
The living and the dead.

Pause

We think with fondness
This Christmas time
Of all those no longer with us
And pray we might keep their memory alive,
Fanning the flame of all that was good
In their spirit and hope.
Amen.

VOICE 3:

The Song of Mary, Luke 1:46–55 paraphrased

We say together in words of Mary:

My soul magnifies the Lord
And my spirit rejoices in my savior.
God looks with favor upon my humility,
And from henceforth all generations shall call me blessed.
The almighty works marvels for me,

One whose name is Holy,
Whose mercy endures from age to age
Upon those who fear divine justice.
God has shown strength of arm,
Shattering the proud in the imagination of their hearts,
Casting the mighty from their thrones
And exalting the lowly.
God has filled the hungry with good things
While the rich have been sent away empty.
The Lord receives my nation as a servant,
Remembering to be merciful
As was promised to our ancestors,
The children of God, forever.

Communion

VOICE 2:
Jesus, the unique heart of our faith,
A heart not of belief but flesh,
Unpredictable, but large enough
To compass all the living and dead.

VOICE 3:
Jesus, the good we see in each other
In human beings of every kind,
In all creatures of water, earth, and sky,
Those known and yet to find.

VOICE 2:
Jesus, the one who cautioned us
That no one is good but God alone,
Who pointed to a realm of justice and peace,
To God's imminent and universal reign.

VOICE 3:
Jesus, whose goodness excelling
Became our example to follow,
Sifting our innermost thoughts and desires,
Captivating through story in every age.

VOICE 2:
Jesus the shepherd king
Who leads us out to a spacious place
And brings out of each their best,
Who to any lengths will go to seek the lost.

VOICE 3:
Jesus, the crucified and resurrected,
Revealing the suffering of God,
Scaling the heights of human altruism
And the depths of God's great love.

VOICE 2:
Jesus, who tested the strength of our endurance
And found it limitless in the palm of God,
Who tested humanity's powers of forgiveness,
Finding them boundless, too.

VOICE 3:
God of forgiveness and reconciliation,
Announce this Christmas a season of amnesty,
Compelling us to put aside our differences,
The grudges we have nursed through the year,
To wipe clean the slate and start anew.

God forgive us
When we have failed to forgive
Those who have offended us
And when we ourselves have inflicted
Suffering on others,
From the kin in our embrace
To the neighbor next door
And all those here and overseas
Whom we have harmed,
Especially those who grow and harvest
And the creatures that become
The food of our feasting.
Help us to minimize

Our impact on the world for ill,
And wherever we can,
To live ethically and considerately
With all.

Pause

VOICE 2:
So we celebrate the life of Christ,
The source of our faith
And its divine incarnation,
With the sharing of a simple meal,
Asking that we as a community
Be like a family that welcomes all
With interest and attentiveness,
Friendship and kindness,
A people unassuming
Who do not let their left hands know
What their right hands are doing
But boast only of the generosity of their God.

VOICE 3:
As Jesus took the bread, he broke it, declaring it to be his body, broken for all the people of the world, that they might know the welcome and goodness of God.

So we, too, take the bread and break it, declaring it to be the body of our church, broken for all the people of the world, that they might know the goodness of God.

As Jesus took the wine, he poured it out, declaring it to be his blood, shed for all the people of the world, that they might know the forgiveness and love of God.

So we, too, take the wine and pour it out, declaring it to be the blood of our church, shed for all the people of the world, that they might know the forgiveness and love of God.

The bread is passed around with the words:

The body of Christ and church, broken for you and for all.

The wine is passed around with the words:

The blood of Christ and church, shed for you and for all.

Voice 2:
All-welcoming, all-loving God,
Wind and breath of Spirit,
Make our church a healer and comforter,
A people and place that liberates,
Enlightens, and transforms,
That gives itself up for the world
Opening up to every sorrow,
Taking them upon itself
And carrying them away,
Just as Christ gave himself up for the world
And bore the pain of sin and death
Inflicted cruelly upon him
So that our guilt and fear might be carried away
In lives of renewed hope
Inspired by Christ's great victory
Over all that is evil
And his revelation of God's amazing love
So a new age could dawn in any moment
From the seeds of the realm of God,
A world where the yoke of all is easy
And our burden ever light.

God of mysteries and marvels,
Fill us with the energy
And radiance of your Spirit.
Be both our great enigma
And our incarnate friend,
That we might recognize you
Whenever you draw near
In every face and form that you assume.

Prayers of Occasion

VOICE 4:
At this time of family and friendship,
Of warmth and hospitality,
We remember especially the lonely,
The outcast, and the destitute,
The deprived and the dispossessed
And all those fallen on hard times
Or lost in depravity and decay.
We leave the door ajar
For any we might meet,
Praying that the poor may find
A place at the banquet
And the lost may find their way back home.

VOICE 5:
We remember in prayer
All those who are unwell this Christmas,
Either in body or in mind,
And proclaim the nearness of God
To the dying and the bereaved.
We remember those who will spend Christmas
In hospitals or nursing homes
And those overseas who yearn for home.
We remember the elderly and the confused,
The downcast and the unloved,
And all who struggle through the winter cold and dark.
We pray for those for whom Christmas
Is clouded by financial worries,
Troubles at work or at home,
Or a seemingly intractable problem,
For all who look toward the New Year
Not with expectation and excitement
But with anxiety and fear:
God be their comfort and strength
Today and throughout the days to come.

VOICE 4:
We remember and pray especially
For those going through divorce or separation,
Nursing their wounds and mourning the loss of a companion,
For all those broken-hearted at a relationship's end,
Those injured and shaken by betrayal or abandonment
And those missing a relative or friend who has died.
We remember all those experiencing the pain of these loses.
God of mercies, in the midst of their grief,
Remind them of your simple comforts.
In the words and welcome of family and friends,
In the beauty of nature and all that it gives us
And in our sustenance day by day,
Reveal to them the vision of a future
Held secure in your loving presence.

VOICE 5:
Saving God, lift the spirits of all the sorrowful
With the kindnesses of neighbor and friend,
With reminders of your blessings past and present,
With the gifts and cards and thoughtful words
Of all those who know them by name,
And may the helping hands and welcoming smiles of strangers
Raise their spirits in new and unexpected ways.

God help us to trust in your past deliverance
And your promise of faithful care,
Even when we cannot feel your presence,
Until the light of our salvation
Flickers once more in the night of our soul.

Meditation on Scripture

VOICE 6:

Feeding the Five Thousand, John 6:1–14

Jesus went to the other side of the Sea of Galilee, also called the Sea of Tiberias. A large crowd kept following him, because they saw the signs that he was doing for the sick. Jesus went up the mountain and

Bible texts for use in the Meditations on Scripture include Matthew 1:18–2:12 and 3:1–12, Mark 1:1–11, Luke 2:1–20 and 3:1–18, John 1:1–34 (Jesus' birth and the proclamations of John the Baptist) or Matthew 14:13–21, Mark 6:30–44, Luke 9:10–17 (Other versions of the feeding of the five thousand) and Mark 8:1–9, Matthew 15:32–39 (The feeding of the four thousand).

sat down there with his disciples. Now the Passover, the festival of the Jews, was near. When he looked up and saw a large crowd coming toward him, Jesus said to Philip, "Where are we to buy bread for these people to eat?" He said this to test him, for he himself knew what he was going to do. Philip answered him, "Six months' wages would not buy enough bread for each of them to get a little." One of his disciples, Andrew, Simon Peter's brother, said to him, "There is a boy here who has five barley loaves and two fish. But what are they among so many people?" Jesus said, "Make the people sit down." Now there was a great deal of grass in the place; so they sat down, about five thousand in all. Then Jesus took the loaves, and when he had given thanks, he distributed them to those who were seated; so also the fish, as much as they wanted. When they were satisfied, he told his disciples, "Gather up the fragments left over, so that nothing may be lost." So they gathered them up, and from the fragments of the five barley loaves, left by those who had eaten, they filled twelve baskets. When the people saw the sign that he had done, they began to say, "This is indeed the prophet who is to come into the world."

Invitation

While the music is playing, you are invited to write your prayer requests or resolutions for the New Year on the decorated scrolls provided. Roll them up again and hang them from the Christmas tree. These can be as simple or detailed as you like, and they can be either signed or anonymous.

Final Prayer and Blessing

VOICE 2:
God of every hour and season,
Of the year's end and its beginning,
Of the summer sun and winter snow
Preside over our Christmas festivities
With shining and infectious joy
While bringing in the lonely,
The grieving, and the sorrowful
Streaming out of the bitter cold
And into the assurance of your love.
Give us all confidence in a future
Filled with opportunities,
Ones you long to help us seize
And make our own.

God of glory and wonder
But most of all of love,
Send us home this Christmas
As peacemakers and healers of wounds.
Make us mindful of the good
More often than the ill
In the familiar faces we have at our sides
And the faces of strangers at the door.
Have us wait with hope
For our prodigals to return home,
Giving up on no one.
Have us return home
Ourselves forgiven.

Sung Refrain

ELEVEN

Sacrifice and Remembrance

The following *Liturgy of Sacrifice and Remembrance* can be used during the period of Lent or on Good Friday and can be referred to as the *Lenten Liturgy of Sacrifice and Remembrance*. It is also suitable for use on national remembrance days. This is a liturgy that mourns with those who mourn. It allows us to give expression to our own experiences of suffering, providing a means for catharsis.

The *Liturgy of Sacrifice* also considers the importance of sacrifice and service in the Christian story and in life in general, in the giving up that allows us to gain what is better. It contemplates the passion of Christ, and in doing so expresses solidarity with all living sentient creatures who suffer. It reminds us of the truth that we gain more from giving and serving others than from receiving and being served by them. This liturgy takes inspiration from the essence and appeal of the Roman Catholic Mass, with its solemn and reverent approach to the long-suffering nature of God. However, it avoids any voyeuristic wallowing in the suffering of others or our own self-indulgence and self-pity. It is instead imbued with the confident message of hope that is the core of the Christian faith and the attitude with which the Christian life should be lived.

The insight that suffering and loss can cultivate wisdom and courage and a total devotion to the other (such as a total trust in God) is key to many religious traditions, but particularly to Christianity. The Christian God is most obviously a suffering God, as epitomized by the torture and death of Jesus, the Incarnation.

This liturgy encourages us to loosen and sometimes let go of the reins in our lives and the lives of others and our churches, and to trust God with the course events will take. Most often the controlling, prescriptive, and intolerant nature of some religious people and institutions comes ironically from their lack of faith, because they do not trust God with the future and are determined to do all they can to make sure things happen the way they, rather than God, think is right and proper. This liturgy reminds us that true faith requires a sacrifice of pride and the courage to keep following in the way of Christ, whatever happens, living fidelity to the way of love and sacrificial service, trusting in God as the source of power and good will, even when it seems to us as if sacrificial service is the surefire road to the churches' demise. Stepping out in faith always involves entering into what is largely unknown, and if it does not seem like that, it probably is something other than faith that one is stepping out in.

It is important, however, to understand that the sacrificial service of wider society, a central purpose of the church and Christian community as a whole, is quite a different thing from the service individual Christians should give to their respective churches. People should not be encouraged to think that they should serve their local church at the expense of their own health, education, career, or family. Neither should they be taught that they cannot take any credit and do not deserve praise or reward for the things they do for the good of the church or community because of some mischievous idea that the good we do is the grace of God working in us alone, and therefore that only some abstract notion of God deserves any praise and reward. These are distortions based on an unhealthy dichotomy between the immanent and transcendent God, and between what is good and what is evil.

It assumes that human beings are entirely evil and that God is either transcendent or indwelling, but is always separate from us in substance: that God is never incarnate in us and we are never one with God in spirit. It is harmful because it opens up the opportunity to exploit those who believe this, those who believe that they have no worth or good in themselves to contribute, and can result in their serving the church without pay, when they need and deserve a source of income, and without acknowledgment or gratitude. It is a way of getting around the laws that ensure people's basic human rights are properly respected.

It is also a way of holding onto an unchallenged leadership by making sure the majority feel inadequate for such tasks. Some churches mistakenly believe that appreciation and praise for the good in people, their gifts, and the good choices they make, will fuel some kind of pride or conceit that will fail to give due credit to God. This, of course, is nonsense, as people are hardly ever known to thank God more than when they have received the admiration and approval of others! It is of utmost importance that people should be paid for church work unless they ask to work for nothing and have an adequate source of income elsewhere.

It is unjust that there should be people working for the church whose income is hardly adequate to cover their basic needs, let alone bring them up to the level of wealth of the majority of the congregation and pastor. Churches should be leading, rather than lagging behind secular society in their ethical standards, including the treatment of those who contribute a great deal of time and energy in maintaining a healthy and successful community. A worker is always worth his or her wages or keep (Matt. 10:10), and workers also deserve praise for what they contribute.

Outstanding achievements should be celebrated with enthusiasm, which has the added effect of inspiring others to do better. Churches must be consistently professional in their dealings with workers, matching and exceeding the standards of secular organizations. There are those who have sadly left churches altogether because they have felt unappreciated and even exploited by institutions that expected much from them but gave little in return. As numbers of independent and self-regulating expressions of church increase, it will become all the more important to remember that social justice and mutual generosity in both material and spiritual matters is the hallmark of any genuinely Christian community.

The following liturgy remembers those who have gone before us, particularly those who have lost their lives as martyrs for a good cause, both in war or peacetime, or through persecution or disaster. It also remembers our own family members and friends who have died. This liturgy honors the war dead while acknowledging the folly and meaninglessness of war and violence. Like all the liturgies, it helps to distill the wisdom of our Christian past and bring to the fore what is most worthy in our inheritance. The liturgy includes prayers for the dead, since these benefit the living and grieving, and because what is past for us may not be past for a God existing outside as well as inside our dimensions of time and space. Even if all that exists were confined to a linear progression through time, those who have passed away may still treasure our prayers, if there is some onward journey of the soul beyond the grave.

In the same way, there is nothing to prevent us from asking them to pray for us, since their souls may be residing in God outside of time or in some other realm. Our ideas about the afterlife, paradise, purgatory, or other processes between death and some ultimate end state are, of course, a combination of speculation and imagination, but the fact that we all die without having reached our own visions of perfection does lead many to believe or hope that further transformation takes place. The key point to make here, however, is that we must each navigate through these issues according to our own spiritual need, imagination, and experience.

One may choose to pray for the dead, just to express affection and goodwill toward them, another to maintain communication with them, and another to pray for their further experience of salvation because of the circumstances surrounding a particular death. A violent, premature, or tragic death, for example, or the death of someone who had been unkind, unpopular, or who committed evil acts (or someone who had not yet forgiven or been forgiven) may understandably engender different responses in the grieving. Yet another person might decide to rest assured that their loved one, safe with God, does not require their prayers and that warm thoughts and treasured memories are enough.

Given the current popularity of mediums and spiritualism in modern times, the lack of prayers with regard to the dead, particularly in the Protestant traditions, has clearly not met the spiritual needs of people who have not yet come to terms with their loss and death's cruel severing of friendship and companionship. Nor have many churches helped people to cope sufficiently with unresolved issues surrounding a death, such as how to come to terms with dreams unfulfilled (in the case of premature death or the death of a child), apologies unspoken, broken relationships unreconciled, characters unimproved, emotions unhealed, or justice unattained or undone in those final days. This liturgy gives acknowledgment and space for those in these situations to express their anger, face their fears, and heal in the assurance of God's love and in the good will and support of all the community.

THE LITURGY OF SACRIFICE
AND REMEMBRANCE

A range of crosses (e.g., Celtic, Roman Catholic, Protestant, and Eastern Orthodox) and depictions of the passion of Christ can be displayed on a central table.

If you would like a relative or friend who has died to be remembered by name during the service, please pass the name to one of the leaders before the service begins. (It may be someone who died recently or someone who died long ago but is presently in your thoughts.)

Sung Refrain

Welcome

VOICE 1:
We come together
With the memories and histories,
The rituals and symbolism
And all that is belonging and home for us,
And we remember the trials
Of our people through the ages,
Recalling their deliverance
Through the power of God,
The God of Jesus
And of his disciples,
A God who suffers like no other,
Who does not shy away

From the ubiquity of pain
Nor the inevitability of death
But one who shows us a way
To meet it with faith and with hope
And to overcome it with love.

All:
May our sufferings teach us compassion,
Deepening our dependence on God
And heightening our devotion,
Making true our love for what is good
And giving rise to wisdom and courage,
For in the best of times we so often disappoint,
While in the worst of times
We might be found at our most noble.
God, help us face our foes with your disarming love,
With the sword of justice and the shield of truth,
And give us strength, through dark of night,
To trust in God and do the right.

VOICE 2:

Poem:
Constancy of Hope

Nothing was there left but hope, for the sun to rise on a better day,
For choked dreams to sing again, the terrors of night away,
Hope there would be some reprieve from the phantom acts of hell,
A time to play and to believe, before the curtains fell.

And hope in splendor stayed afloat, steamed on no strength for turning.
It kept me from the Devil's trust, my dying soul from burning,
And though adversity prevailed, hope strove to do the right,
A vestige of my fading will, still standing in the fight.

I waited out my agonies, like Jesus in the garden,
Saying, "Why have you forsaken me, deprived me your pardon?"
But time would bring the Comforter, the Spirit of my healing,
And there would see a miracle, that place where I was kneeling.

For soon did come a time to sing, of God's redeeming love
And stories told of sacrifice, of Jesus crowned in blood,
Nothing kept and nothing spared but poured out for us all,
This love amazing, love divine, that once was sorrowful.

For as I suffered, God was there incarnate once again,
And in my emptiness complete, there shone my greatest gain.
For like the king upon the cross, my crown was resurrection,
And nothing then could frighten me, but the glare of God's perfection.

O give me strength to tread the path that leads beyond our knowing,
Where the fallen light the way, their tears no longer flowing.
Take my hand and guide me when I'm deaf and cannot see,
When the Devil's kingdom sparkles and I'm tempted there to flee.

Christ, O Christ of souls reborn in mortal life and after,
Cast the shadows of the past away beyond the rafter.
Read once more the letters of God's love, my only treasure,
Telling how it suffers all, so life will bring us pleasure.

The heads of poppies whisper names of those who once were brave,
And all the spirits of our dead are remembered in the nave,
Hope for them and hope for us in Jesus there to find
In one who lived and died and rose immortal for our kind.

Invitation

While the music is playing, you are invited to light a candle as a symbol of enduring hope for yourself, your loved ones present and deceased, and for the world.

VOICE 1:
We look to the hills with expectancy
For the coming of our God,
The hand of salvation to heal us,
For it reaches out to touch the earth,
To soothe the aching of the land
And the groaning of the ocean.
For the victor lifts her shield to defend us
And calms the threatening storm.

She leads us like a shepherd to the lake
Where every soul may drink its fill.

God of wonders, whose name is holy
Beyond all words and speech,
Raise in our midst
The cities, gardens and wildernesses of your realm
By the workings of a mighty will
That earth may be united with heaven
And each may eat and drink in peace
And sleep undisturbed in their own land,
For all debts will be forgiven
And the lions shall lie with the lambs.
Yes, all will be delivered from evil and temptation
And none shall be made afraid,
Because yours is a holy cosmos,
The power, and the glory
Of creation restored to health and balance,
And of life sustained forever.

Prayers of Occasion

VOICE 3:
We thank God
For all those who strive against evil,
Upholding the rights and dignity of the vulnerable,
Those who feed and clothe the poor and exploited,
And all who choose to live and work
For the benefit of others as much as themselves,
Especially those men and women
Prepared to make the greatest of sacrifices
Even unto death for the sake of others.
May their immense bravery
Bring them honor and blessing,
And may they inspire us all
To follow in the path of Christ,
Who shows us the way to life.

We remember in particular
All our armed forces:

Merciful God, remove our greed far from us
So our descendants may know nothing of war,
Of the folly and waste of that insatiable beast
That rears its head so often between us.
Be at the front line of all our conflicts
With soldier, medic, chaplain, and civilian,
And behind it, with those who fear, and those who mourn.
Make our church powerful for the realm of God,
A wrench in the wheels of un-grace,
So that we may reclaim heaven.
Give us a love that suffers no evil,
Whose warmth reaches to the ends of the earth.
Lead us, O Christ, to the way ahead
And flood it with your light.

Meditation on Scripture

VOICE 4:

The Beatitudes, Matthew 5:1–12

When Jesus saw the crowds, he went up the mountain; and after he sat down, his disciples came to him. Then he began to speak, and taught them, saying:

"Blessed are the poor in spirit, for theirs is the kingdom of heaven.
"Blessed are those who mourn, for they will be comforted.
"Blessed are the meek, for they will inherit the earth.
"Blessed are those who hunger and thirst for righteousness,
        for they will be filled.
"Blessed are the merciful, for they will receive mercy.
"Blessed are the pure in heart, for they will see God.
"Blessed are the peacemakers,
for they will be called children of God.
"Blessed are those who are persecuted for righteousness' sake,
for theirs is the kingdom of heaven.

Bible texts for use in the Meditations on Scripture include Luke 18:9–14 (The Pharisee and the tax collector), Matthew 4:1–11, Luke 4:1–13 (The temptation of Jesus), any of the accounts of Jesus' crucifixion and death in the Gospels such as Mark 15:21–41, Matthew 27:32–56, and Luke 23:26–49, or passages such as Matthew 6:5–18 (Concerning prayer and fasting), Matthew 6:1–4 (Concerning almsgiving), and Matthew 6:19–21 (Concerning treasures).

"Blessed are you when people revile you and persecute you and utter all kinds of evil against you falsely on my account. Rejoice and be glad, for your reward is great in heaven, for in the same way they persecuted the prophets who were before you."

Invitation

As the music is playing, you are invited to receive a cross of ash on your forehead from a leader as a sign and reminder of your mortality, your unity with Christ in death, and belonging to Christ in life.

The leader can use the words "Be one with Christ in life and death" when administering the cross of ash.

Prayers for the Dead

VOICE 1:
Let us pray for those who walked this way before us,
Born of spirit within a God of spirit,
Our family members and friends,
Those who died recently and long ago
We remember by name. . . .
We ask that they receive our earthly blessings
In the language of angels
And know of our persistent love,
For it reaches well beyond the grave
And ascends in prayer to the heavens.

We share our lives in prayer
With all our deceased
And sense that they are still with us,
For God is here, and they that are passed,
Subsumed in God, are somehow near.
May they know everlasting peace
And the grace of Christ, our host
Exceeding the justice of humankind
With mercy inconceivable.
Remember them, our incarnate hope,
And remember us all
When you come into your realm.

VOICE 3:
 Merciful God, we bring before you
All the pain of relationships unhealed
And broken still at the point of death,
Forgiveness not yet given or received,
Apologies unspoken and unheard,
Lost time not yet made up
Characters unimproved and unrepentant,
And justice unattained or undone.
May the living and the dead find peace
Knowing that your love and forgiveness are enough
And that all is reconciled in oneness with God.
Where amends might still be made in life,
May all pride and fear be overcome
Before the hour of grace is gone.
We pray for those whose dreams for the future
Will never be fulfilled,
For those taken prematurely or in youth,
In sickness, tragic accident, or wanton violence,
Remembering all who love and miss them,
Who weep for all that they might have been.
We bring to you all our anger
For deaths that seem untimely and unjust

And all the force of our grief,
Knowing that you hear and receive it,
That you are familiar with our distress
With every troubled detail of our lives,
And long to make them right.

VOICE 1:
Though in our mortal lives
We will never comprehend
How and why good and evil coexist,
Why the latter goes unbanished from reality
By a God so powerful and just,
We nonetheless accept that, God,
You are worthy of all our trust,
For you are goodness itself,
The overwhelming nemesis of every evil
That blights the earth and humankind,
And time itself will give you vindication.
The tenacity of truth will be your proof
For our memories of your rescue in the past
That even when long waited for, would always come,
Will fill us once again with confidence,
Revealing your steadfast and unfailing love,
Love that lies behind our every wall of tears
No matter how little we can see,
And those things that confound us now,
Creating in us our doubts,
You will one day elucidate,
That day when we enter once more
Your most secret of places,
That place within your very heart
From where it was that we first came.

Communion

VOICE 3:
We approach the table of the God of sacrifice,
Where Jesus prepared to give himself up

For the greater good of humanity
And asked to be remembered thereafter
By all his disciples through the ages.
So we honor his memory
And all that he gave
By following his instruction
In our breaking of bread
And our pouring of wine
And also by offering our lives daily
In actions small or great,
Following the way of the cross,
For in every gain there is sacrifice
In every achievement, toil,
And in every love, loss.

May the Communion table remind us
To give freely and cheerfully,
For giving is the path that ends in blessing
And brings joy along the way.

VOICE 1:
In the upper room among his friends
Jesus blessed the food that would nourish their bodies
And the symbols that would nourish their souls
As reminders of all he lived and taught
And of his final sacrifice.
For in the depths of divine love
Would be the greatest loss of all.

Lifting the bread:

"This is my body," Jesus declared, "broken for you."

Lifting the wine:

"And this is my blood, poured out for you."

Take, eat and drink of a new way of life,
Accepting the invitation of Jesus
To become one with him in flesh and blood,

Sealing a new covenant of mercy and love.

The bread is distributed with the words:
The body of Christ, a pledge of mercy.

The wine is shared with the words:
The blood of Christ, a pledge of love.

VOICE 3:
Jesus became a final sacrifice
So his people could enjoy the favor of God
Without the letting of blood
And the destruction of life,
And though there would be those
Who would give their lives
For the sake of his cause,
It was not demanded of them
But only given willingly,
As Jesus gave willingly.
For Jesus came to show us
That we might gain life,
Not from grasping but by losing it,
Letting go of the self
And seeking first the righteousness
And the realm of God,
Trusting God with our future,
For life is not a number of years
But is to be found instead
In the strength of our hope,
In the depth of our faith
And the breadth of our love.

So I give my voice to sing
The stories of our God
And my heart to be filled
With all God's love.
I give my mind to know
All the riches of God's truth

And my life to find
Her treasures everlasting.

Final Prayer and Blessing

VOICE 1:
God beyond order and chaos,
Beyond the existing and impossible
And all the planes of our knowing,
Speak into our consciousness
In languages of the earth
Your translations of the glories
Of new worlds and divine.
Distill them into words we can command,
Words of faith, words of hope, and words of love.

VOICE 3:
Send us out in generosity of spirit
And in thoughtfulness of mind,
In mellowness of heart
And in timelessness of soul,
Giving as you have given,
Loving as you have loved,
Becoming as you have forever been.

May our meditations plant seeds
Of insight and discernment,
Of gentleness and honesty.
May they replenish the soils of the spirit
With waters of relief,
With clarity and hope.
May they bloom with prayer
And flower with kindness.

Sung Refrain

TWELVE

Meditations for Worship and Well-Being

Meditation is an art in the sense that it can only be appreciated through experience and mastered through practice, rather than by theorizing. However, there is nothing mysterious about the form of meditation taught here. It is a logical method based on reason and observation. This short chapter is written to give you the necessary tools to lead or participate in guided meditations which will help to support spiritual formation by enabling you to get the best out of the liturgies in this book and any other worship materials you may use.

This guide to meditation concentrates, in particular, on the human habit or condition of fear because I believe it to be far more significant among the common impediments to our well-being and spiritual growth than has been hitherto acknowledged. Fear causes prolonged stress which results in unhelpful thought patterns and behaviors, mood swings, and depression. Most of us experience these adverse effects of fear over the course of our lives.

By spiritual growth, formation, or development, I mean the deepening and broadening of our understanding of divinity, of religion, theology, and ethics, and of our understanding of the physical world (including our bodies and brains) and its complex interactions with the meanings, principles, and purposes that faith may ascribe to it. Spiritual progress is marked by the cultivation of wisdom: a sophisticated moral sense, a creative and transformative way of life, and a healthy conception of God.

These meditations are written for personal use, but they can be easily adapted for use in a guided or group meditation. However, in the latter case, it is important to mention that whoever leads the meditations should be at the very least experienced in leading reflective worship so that problems with articulation or maintaining the rhythm, pace, and correct emphasis do not detract from the group's experience of contemplation and insight.

Overcoming Inertia

Inertia in various degrees is a universal human weakness. We all make ourselves comfortable with the familiar and resist change. In fact, almost all of us would have to admit that we are to some degree innately lazy, with a tendency to choose the path of least resistance even when there is a better path in sight. Most of us will even be able to name people we know to be stuck in a rut and far too cozy with the situation there are in, however unsatisfactory that may be and how-ever much they might complain about it.

Such people would rather not take the risk of changing it, even if such a change could significantly improve their quality of life. Some of us may even have to admit that we number among these people. The reason I am writing about inertia is because any process that leads to spiritual maturity demands, first and foremost, that the pil-grim or student of the way commit wholeheartedly to change and transformation, to self-improvement and the enhancement of the environment they are passing through. This subsection should get you into the right frame of mind for commencing one of the medita-tions that follow.

The way of life that succumbs to inertia leads only to stagnation and bitterness. It is always best to take action to change an unhealthy or unfulfilling aspect of your life, because such situations inevitably deteriorate and prompt action is always better than a forced reaction once things have become entrenched. It is important to remember that there is always a way to overcome inertia. All those excuses about the importance of security, safety, financial restraints, and lack of con-fidence are just that, excuses.

They may even betray a cowardly trait that is bound to bring you nothing but feelings of shame and regret. There will always be an affordable step with reasonable risk that you can take to improve your situation if you really want to find it. If you are honest with yourself, you will acknowledge that many people before you, perhaps even family members and friends, have taken the decisions you have been vacillating about, made the changes that you have been hesitating to make, and have prospered as a result. If you are one of these people, you will need to stop procrastinating and understand that any unfortunate consequences of a new step you might take will be far more bearable than the self-loathing you will feel if you allow yourself to waste your life sinking deeper into that rut.

You also need to trust that you have many more resources, abilities, and strengths than you are generally aware of, and that in reality, coping with change will be much easier than you think. You will have met the kind of person who is twisted with resentment and takes out on others the guilt they have regarding their own lack of success in life. Do you want to be one of them, or would you rather end up as someone who acknowledges that they have made some mistakes, maybe even a few major ones, but whose decisive action resulted overall in a life of achievement, adventure, and satisfaction?

So go ahead and start that new exercise regime or cut out that junk food and those long hours in front of unedifying television. Go ahead and apply for that new job, pursue that interest, or retrain for that new career. Go ahead and join the local sports team or the political movement you care about. Join that dating site or ask that man or woman you like out for a drink. What have you got to lose apart from that little bit of false pride that assumes you are universally employable, likable, good at politics, good at sports, or attractive, and so on, if they say no or you do not succeed? Start practicing meditation and allowing yourself to heal from past and present trauma, disappointment, betrayal or whatever it is that holds you back. Do not lie in bed watching your life go by like a bad dream you cannot wake up from. Get out there and chase your waking dreams instead.

Practicing Mindfulness

This is a form of meditation which allows the mind to find a place of calm by increasing our awareness of both our outer and inner reality. It reveals the deceptions we have been laboring under and the unhelpful emotional responses and habits of thought we have all picked up over the years. When practiced regularly these meditations can alleviate stress, discomfort, tension, and pain. They are also extremely valuable in the treatment of mild to moderate anxiety, panic disorders, phobia, and depression. They can still be effective in very severe cases but may need to be practiced in conjunction with other treatments. Meditation needs to be practiced regularly, and it is important not to be impatient with time. Initially set aside at least half an hour each day to meditate and then gradually practice it at other times during the day until awareness begins to become a natural state of mind.

If you are looking to recover from a state of grief, depression, or anxiety, it may well take several months before you are completely well again, so patient practice is essential. For those who are starting off in a healthier place, or for those who have recovered but would like to learn techniques for remaining so, it can still take several months of practice to master this form of meditation, and much longer to perfect it. Whatever the emotional and psychological state you are in at this time, meditation can improve your quality of life and well-being both physically and spiritually.

Some people may see results almost immediately, while others may have a longer journey with a number of setbacks. It is important that you persevere, as the results are worth the wait. Freedom from unhealthy patterns of thought and emotion, and wrong beliefs about oneself, others, the world, and God, can transform your life, including your prayer and worship life. Meditation can show you a way to be kinder to yourself, which in turn allows you to be kinder to others and able to respect and love them better. It is a priceless tool to employ in one's personal efforts at spiritual growth and devotion. Meditation helps us to see God for what or who God really is and then to love God better as a result.

Below are the three essential awareness meditations that you can begin practicing. Make sure you have at least an hour to spare before beginning any of these meditations, even if you intend on meditating only for thirty minutes, so that you will not feel rushed or anxious about finishing on time. Use an alarm so that you do not run over your allotted time and make yourself stressed by being late for something or getting inadequate sleep.

Start by making yourself comfortable by adjusting your posture if necessary. It is best to position yourself so that you are neither too rigid nor in any way hunched over. You do not want to be so comfortable that you fall asleep or so upright that your muscles will give up halfway through. You will find your own happy medium with practice. There is no position that can be recommended universally as our bodies are all different shapes and in different conditions to begin with. What may be a comfortable position for one person may be painful or even impossible for another, as many who have tried the traditional lotus position of the Indian Hindu and Buddhist contemplatives have discovered. Such advanced positions can require a great deal of practice and patience to get used to.

Situational Awareness

Gradually turn your attention to your surroundings. With only small and slow movements of the eyes, start to take in the sights around you. Notice details of which you were previously unaware. Then notice the sounds. Become aware of natural rhythms, like that of your own or a neighbor's breathing, or the patter of rain outside. Then notice any smells, perhaps the lingering smell of that morning's coffee or the perfume or aftershave you used. Finally, begin to notice the feeling of the chair beneath you, the floor beneath your feet, the clothing you are wearing and even any movement of the air around you. Take your time with each of these steps. Take as long as you need to deepen your awareness beyond what you have achieved before. Maintain this awareness until the end of your meditation, allowing it to deepen but gently drawing your attention back to your surroundings if it drifts to some internal thought or concern, which doubtless it will do often at first.

After some time, you may notice that you have a habit of rating the sights, sounds, smells, and feelings around you as ugly or beautiful, pleasant or unpleasant, interesting or uninteresting. Move your attention slowly from one thing to another and notice these responses to the information that is constantly flowing in through your senses from the outside world. The responses are so quick they seem almost to be automatic. Notice them but do not dwell on them. Gently move your attention from one thing to another. Do not worry about the judgments, thoughts, and feelings this information generates. Just observe them.

As you begin to see, smell, hear, or feel things in more detail, and as you notice your habitual reactions to them, you will begin to see the things set apart from the categories you are so quick to ascribe them to. You will begin to see them as they really are. You will begin to see that most things are neither beautiful nor ugly, good nor bad, pleasant nor unpleasant. They do not require the extent of thought or the degree of emotional response, whether positive feelings of pleasure or negative feelings such as irritation, which you have been in the habit of attaching to them. They simply ARE.

By meditating, you will learn to view the world as if you are seeing it for the very first time, as though you are seeing it through the eyes of a newborn child.

Body Awareness

Gradually turn your attention to your body. Slowly, beginning with your feet and toes, tense the muscles as far as possible for a slow count of five, then let them relax at their own natural pace. Gradually work your way up your body, tensing and relaxing muscles until you reach the muscles of the forehead and scalp. As you allow your muscles to relax on their own, explore the sensation of deeper and deeper relaxation. It is important to include the muscles that are particularly affected by stress and most likely to be tense, such as the muscles of the forehead and face (especially around the eyes and jaw), the stomach and abdominal muscles, and the shoulder and neck muscles. In order to tense specific muscles fully you may need to bend or extend or press that part of your body against whatever you are sitting or lying on.

The use of deliberate tension wearies the muscles so that when they relax they relax more fully, sending signals to your brain which indicate this. By reminding your brain of how the extremes of tension and relaxation in the muscles feel and the contrast between them, you will become more aware of areas of the body where you are in the habit of holding onto unnecessary tension. As your awareness grows you can use this technique to let the tension go and discover the soft feeling in the muscles that is characteristic of the relaxed state.

In a time of stillness and quiet, begin to notice any other sensations in your body. Notice also your reactions to these sensations. Most of you will find that you are in the habit of attaching emotions to them, recoiling from anything that feels irritating or uncomfortable and trying to hold onto or reproduce sensations that feel pleasurable or soothing. Just notice this happening and observe the sensations in increasing detail as they come and go. If an unpleasant sensation and the negative emotional response to it is persistent—an itch, for example—do not worry.

This is a very common experience. Simply let the sensation and emotions be there. Resist the urge to change position, scratch the itch, and so on. Only adjust your position if you are really in pain. However irritating a sensation or unpleasant the emotion it stirs, let them be there. Observe them as they are. You will also notice that your efforts to reproduce or hold onto positive sensations and the emotions they engender are largely unsuccessful. Simply let these pleasant sensations be there for as long as they naturally last. Do not continue trying to reproduce or hold onto them.

If you are suffering from stress and anxiety, notice and explore its symptoms, the uneasy feeling or feelings of panic, palpitations, and sweating, shallow breaths or the inability to take deep breaths, blurred vision, trembling, itching, tingling and numbness, or the myriad of other symptoms that an excess of adrenaline and overbreathing due to stress can cause. Observe each detail of these sensations as they arise. There is no need to worry about them, as they are completely normal symptoms of stress. (Always see your doctor if you are worried about your symptoms, to rule out any other causes and to put your mind at rest.) The nervous system has a remarkable ability to heal itself when it is allowed to do so, and you will allow it to heal if you simply allow those sensations to be there without fearing them or trying to run from them toward various distractions.

Stand back from your sensations and their associated emotions as far as possible. In your mind walk further and further away from them. Then come forward again and peer closely at them, studying their detail, how they arise and how they fade away, before moving away again. Repeat this several times. You will begin to see how most of these sensations are neither as euphoric (in the positive case) nor as frightening (in the negative case) as you once thought. Most of them simply are.

Learn to experience sensations as they really are. Observe your body as if you were aware of it for the first time.

Mind Awareness

Gradually begin to notice the constant stream of thoughts passing through your mind. There may be images or imaginings attached to these thoughts. Notice these also.

You will notice some of these thoughts are rational and some are irrational, some you deem to be negative, some positive, some ordinary, some bizarre, some pleasant, some disturbing. Notice the categories into which you place your thoughts and note the positive and negative emotions you attach to these thoughts, and images. Notice just how quick you are to attach positive and negative values and emotions to every thought and image that enters your mind.

Do not be concerned about any of your thoughts or imaginings, whatever they are. We all have plenty of thoughts and imaginings we would be ashamed or embarrassed to share with others. Just observe them and let them pass.

Stand back from this stream of thought and emotion. Do not try to reject negative thoughts or emotions. Do not try to hold on to positive ones. Simply watch them all flow by. Some thoughts or images might stick in the mind a bit longer, or they might resurface repeatedly. Do not be concerned about sticky, repetitive, or intrusive thoughts, even if the thoughts are negative and an unpleasant emotion is attached to them. Let both the thought and the emotion be there. They can do you no harm. Even the most negative thoughts, imaginings or images in the mind are powerless. Let them be there for as long as they last.

If you tend toward frequent negative thoughts or depression, observe those thoughts and the attached emotions such as hopelessness or despair. Let them be there. Watch them from a distance and do not get involved with them by analyzing or worrying about them. Your subconscious constantly throws up thoughts and images into the conscious mind, but the subconscious is not within your immediate control, so struggling to get rid of negative thoughts is a futile effort that only produces more stress.

Doing so will only activate a vicious cycle, because as you increase your emotional response of frustration with those thoughts and images, your subconscious mind will perceive them as more and more important and will throw them up into your conscious mind increasingly often. This process has evolved as a warning system to protect you from real dangers, since those real dangers illicit the greatest emotional responses but unfortunately this system commonly malfunctions and we end up obsessing about things that do not require such attention. You can indirectly affect the subconscious to some degree by monitoring what you expose your mind to in terms of the media you watch or the company you keep. This is well worth doing, but it takes time for memories and images to fade, and for now it is best to allow whatever is in your mind to be there without worrying about it.

If the thought and your immediate emotional response is, in contrast, positive or pleasurable, do not try to hold onto it or retrieve it when it passes. Just let it be there for however long it naturally lasts. The frustration that will ensue if you try to engineer or grasp thoughts and emotions which are naturally fleeting will soon drain away any pleasure or happiness they once gave you. They are just like the flower that, once picked, quickly loses its bloom.

Do not be concerned or frightened by unusually intense emotions accompanying thoughts or images, or emotions which seem disproportionate to the situation or facts. Just notice your emotional habits and let each feeling pass, with the intensity and duration it needs.

Begin to observe your thoughts and emotions from a distance. Gradually increase that distance. Then come close and study how they rise and how they pass away before walking away again. You will begin to see that they are neither as pleasant in the positive cases, nor as frightening or depressing in the negative ones as you once thought them to be.

Look at your mind as if you were seeing it for the first time. Learn to accept and observe your thoughts and emotions as they are.

Notes on the Meditations

You will notice how much emotional and nervous energy you are attaching to thoughts, emotions, sensations, and information coming in through your senses. You will notice how many of those sights, sounds, smells, feelings, sensations, and thoughts are in fact neutral and do not deserve or require the judgments, emotions, or mental categories you assign them to. You will notice just how many intriguing and marvelous things you do not ordinarily notice because you are in the habit of subconsciously overlooking them, deeming them to be unimportant, because they do not trigger any emotional response.

During meditations you may become aware that you have been misled or deceived regarding yourself, others, God, or the world around you. You may uncover irrationality, particularly superstitions, and false beliefs. Meditation has allowed you to identify these things, and once identified they gradually lose their influence over you and you gain a more accurate perspective on yourself and everything else. You begin to see how you were misled and will not be so easily deceived in the future.

You may have noticed that you have become sensitized to your own thoughts, bodily sensations, environment, and emotions and have been caught up in vicious cycles or feedback loops of unhelpful thoughts triggering emotions which in turn reinforce the unhelpful thoughts and so on. To reconnect with reality you must learn to observe these at a distance. This will eventually allow the passions that are fueling these cycles to drain away. Gradually the negative thoughts will become less frequent, as they are no longer of importance to you, and the emotions attached to them will lessen in intensity.

Equally, the fleeting positive feelings attached to thoughts and information coming in through the senses will be gradually replaced by a more permanent, more satisfying state of calm that is much better for your nerves and your health in general and is a truer experience of happiness or contentment. You will not lose your sense of wonder, your feelings of love and pleasure, and your appreciation of beauty; indeed, you will deepen your experience of all of these, because they will no longer be obscured, cut short, or tainted by the uncomfortable effects of adrenaline produced by grasping at such things, nor will they lead you to unhelpful or unhealthy behavioral excesses such as addiction, rashness, or extreme risk taking as they might have done before.

Keep practicing and you will find a peace and balance in life where your perceptions, thoughts, and emotions are in step with reality. If you began meditations in a stressed or anxious state, you will gradually find that as your emotions settle down your nervous system has the chance to recover and resume normal, or produce better-than-normal, responses to your thoughts and the environment and the experiences you have. You will learn by practicing meditation to achieve a state of bright alertness but without any of the tension and stress that used to accompany it.

It is only a matter of time before you are able to perceive things around you and within you AS THEY REALLY ARE.

There will always be occasional moments where your nerves catch you unawares and negative emotions grip you in a rush of adrenaline even before you have had time to think about the situation or event they are responding to. However, with the techniques of meditation you will have learned how to sit comfortably and patiently with these emotions rather than be disturbed or carried away by them, and you may even be able to harness their energy in creating something positive and new.

Facing Fear

Learning to acknowledge, accept, and then to conquer your fears is a vital part of coping and succeeding in life. There is no way you can go through life fulfilling your potential while completely avoiding what you are afraid of. There will be scary and nerve-wracking moments in any relationship, career, and leisure pursuit. Moreover, there is certainly no way of escaping the inevitable fate of illness and ultimately your own demise, both of which are common sources of fear, dread, and insecurity.

The meditations above will help you to face your fears by learning to see them for what they really are, no more no less: just passing feelings, sensations, and thoughts. They will also give you the tools to identify and break any cycles where you are feeding your fears by adding the fear of fear into the mix. However, practicing meditations and coming to a point where you feel more in control is not enough on its own. You need to prove to yourself that all those hours of self-improvement in solitude have enabled you to live a better and fuller life. You need to confront the challenges of your work, social, and private life head on without forgetting what you have learned and reverting to the bad habits of the past. The mind-set you are developing through meditation should be sustained throughout each week and should be evident to others in ordinary life if real progress is being made.

As simple way to start integrating awareness meditation into your daily life, especially to combat fear and nerves, is simply to keep reminding yourself to slow down and become aware of your surroundings, body, thoughts, and emotions without judging them. Then you will realize just how much of life is simply neutral rather than awe- or fear-inspiring. Another helpful suggestion is to take up yoga, ballet, tai chi, or some other physical discipline that requires slow graceful movements, as practicing slow and graceful movements of the body encourages slow and graceful movements of the mind.

Do not let fear be a factor in deciding what you do in life. Do what you know is right or what you need to do to pursue your dreams, even if you know you will experience fear in the process. Avoidance and distraction promise much comfort but ultimately deliver very little. Do not put your trust in them.

Do not give yourself the time for an overanalysis of any given situation. Just get yourself to that dance, drive over that wobbly bridge, take that speaking engagement, perform for that crowd, and throw yourself out of that plane (without forgetting your parachute of course!). Do not stew in your own negative thinking when you awake in the morning; it will only escalate. Instead, nip it in the bud by getting up and using your muscles. It may well be the case that you currently do a lot of things that you would never have dared to do years ago, so you have your own proof that overcoming fear is not just possible but essential

If you suffer severely from anxiety or depression or both, a book that can help you all the way to recovery, which I highly recommend and which inspired my meditation techniques, is *Self-Help for Your Nerves: Learn to Relax and Enjoy Life Again by Overcoming Stress and Fear* by Dr. Claire Weekes, MBE, MB, DSc, FRACP (London: Thorsons, 1995). Her other works and Pacific Recordings can also be obtained online. I also recommend David Johnson's Freedom from Fear Recovery Program (based on Weekes's methods), which can be obtained at *www.panicfree.co.nz/*, where there is also a forum for sufferers to support one another. There is also a charity called Anxiety Free International, which uses the method of Claire Weekes and the recordings of David Johnson and which will be able to provide support in the future.

in expressing your full personality and talents. You have to do things in spite of the shaking hands, pounding heart, and racing thoughts, even if at first you feel it's not you doing it let alone enjoying it, and that your body has to take over on automatic pilot. The more you do it using the techniques of meditation, and the more your body learns that its dramatic fear response is unnecessary, the more comfort you will feel and the easier it will become.

You will soon feel like the owner of your body again and the activity that once scared you will become just another thing that you do as part of your normal routine. You may well even enjoy it. Your fear may always be with you to a lesser degree if you are about to speak or perform in public or take part in an extreme sport because, after all, these are difficult tasks which pose a real threat either to one's dignity or one's person should they go awry. In fact, having a bit of nervous energy may help you to work harder and perform better. However, with the help of meditation, it will no longer be unpleasant enough to discourage you and will be greatly outweighed by the satisfaction of the job well done.

If you are in the grip of an unusually intense and irrational fear such as agoraphobia or health anxiety, or if your life is impeded by a phobia, such as the fear of heights, birds, or buttons, or whatever it may be, you need to practice the meditations above regularly and carefully until you can introduce these techniques to activities which force you to confront your particular fear. Face your fear, however intense it feels (the feelings can't hurt you!), and accept the way your body responds.

Slow down and imagine you are floating through the activity. Understand that the fear and panic you are feeling has nothing much to do with the activity itself, the outside world, the physical symptom, the bird or button itself, and so on. It is just a learned physical response which has become an ingrained habit but which can be unlearned.

Sometimes the initial cause of a fear was a disturbing experience including that specific object or situation early in life or a response learned from a parent who had the same habit of fear. However, very often the object of the fear is completely random. Free-floating anxiety simply landed on that particular thing arbitrarily. For example, it may just so happen that at a time in your life when you feel insecure or frightened, you are in a busy, crowded space, and thus your brain begins to associate those anxious feelings with that circumstance and every time you thenceforth enter a busy, crowded place, as a consequence, those same feelings come rushing back.

You are, however, not frightened of busy, crowded spaces; you are frightened of that feeling your body is in the habit of reproducing whenever you visit such places. It is important to remember that it is not the thing in itself you are afraid of (unless of course it is actually a real threat to you, like a deadly poisonous spider crawling up your leg). It is therefore not the trigger activity or object, but just those harmless feelings of fear you have to face up to and learn to live with and accept for a time. You will find the feelings gradually diminish in intensity and then disappear altogether of their own accord.

This advice is not just good for those with a particular irrational fear. It is also good to learn to stay calm in the face of real threats like that poisonous spider. Our natural fear responses are useful for fight or flight but they often get in the way of more helpful measured responses. Try fighting or running with that spider on your leg and you will most likely be bitten, because you will terrify the little creature.

Meditation, facing your fear, accepting fear, and floating through it is a useful response for us all to learn.

If you have a specific and seemingly intractable problem—for example, something to do with finances, family, or an untreatable health problem that is causing you stress—always seek advice from a person qualified in the relevant area, such as a lawyer, doctor, or debt counselor so that you can find a means of managing and coping with the problem in the best way possible. Additionally, you can seek support and encouragement from your local minister, if you have one you know and trust. Such people will have received several years of training and gained valuable experience which will help you to navigate your way through a difficult problem or period in your life. They may also have further contacts who might give more expert assistance. If possible, especially if you are in a vulnerable state, always seek advice from someone who does not have an ulterior motive or agenda in helping you and who is unlikely to impose inflexible opinions or advice on you which would only increase your anxieties. The only thing that remains is to wish you well with your meditations and spiritual growth, and to entrust my liturgies to God and to all those who will read and make use of them.

About the Author

ANASTASIA SOMERVILLE-WONG grew up in London (England) before moving to Scotland to study philosophy and politics at the University of Edinburgh. After her graduation she spent three years working for charities and in social work and administration before studying for a PhD in divinity with the University of Aberdeen on the subject of George Fielden MacLeod's Christian social vision. She has a decade of experience working with adults and young people in churches of a variety of denominations and in the role of a lay church leader, teacher, and speaker. She has recently been working as a writer and poet, a consultant community researcher, and a lecturer in the history of Christianity.

Other Books from The Pilgrim Press

TOUCH HOLINESS
Resources for Worship, Updated
Ruth C. Duck and Maren C. Tirabassi
ISBN 978-0-8298-1908-3/paper/304 pages/$22

Over the years, the words written by Duck and Tirabassi have impacted and transformed hundreds of thousands of worshippers. In 1990, *Touch Holiness* made its debut and rapidly became the bestselling worship resource published by The Pilgrim Press to date. Now, over twenty years later, Duck and Tirabassi have merged new liturgies with the best of the old.

GIFTS IN OPEN HANDS
Maren C. Tirabassi and Kathy Wonson Eddy
ISBN 978-0-8298- 1839-0/paper/320 pages/$28

Gifts in Open Hands was inspired by the bestselling *Gifts of Many Cultures: Worship Resources for the Global Community*, also by Tirabassi and Eddy (1995, United Church Press). This fresh new edition, like the previous, contains a wealth of multicultural liturgies, prayers, affirmations, blessings, and poetry by people from the global community. These beautifully written pieces can be used in worship and celebration of sacraments, sacred seasons, and all other occasions in the life of the church.

BEFORE THE AMEN
Creative Resources for Worship
Maren Tirabassi and Maria Tirabassi
ISBN 978-0-8298-1750-8/paper/262 pages/$20

This book is a worship anthology that evolved from the bestselling title *Touch Holiness: Resources for Worship* (The Pilgrim Press, 1990). Providing fresh language inclusive of gender, ethnicity, race, age, orientation, and ability, this book contains nine chapters of seasonal materials, three chapters of sacraments and services, and seven chapters oriented by topic. It is filled with materials that come before amen such as: resources for the worship service (readings, healing services, and chancel dramas); general resources; and prayers for special issues such as natural disasters, domestic violence, and surrogate parents.

GIFTS OF MANY CULTURES
Worship Resources for the Global Community
Maren C. Tirabassi and Kathy Wonson Eddy
ISBN 0-8298-1029-3/paper/260 pages/$28

Filled with a moving collection of liturgical resources from the global community, *Gifts of Many Cultures* will enrich the worship life of congregations in all denominations. Tirabassi and Eddy have developed an anthology of original prayers, poetry, stories, and readings for: sermons; invocations; calls to worship; confessions; and liturgies for Holy Communion and baptism; guided meditations, songs, drawings; and other resources designed around the seasons of the church year.

To order these or any other books from
The Pilgrim Press
call or write:

The Pilgrim Press
700 Prospect Avenue East
Cleveland, Ohio 44115-1100

Phone orders: 1-800-537-3394
Fax orders: 216-736-2206

Please include shipping charges of $7.00
for the first book and $1.00 for each additional book.

Or order from our web sites at
www.thepilgrimpress.com
and www.uccresources.com.

Prices subject to change without notice.